HERMES BOOKS

John Herington, General Editor

HOMER

PAOLO VIVANTE

YALE UNIVERSITY PRESS
NEW HAVEN AND LONDON

PA
4037
·V49
1985

Designed by Sally Harris
and set in Palatino type by
Brevis Press, Bethany, Connecticut.
Printed in the United States of America by
Vail-Ballou Press, Binghamton, New York.

Library of Congress Cataloging in Publication Data

Vivante, Paolo.
    Homer.

    (Hermes books)
    Bibliography: p.
    Includes index.
    1. Homer—Criticism and interpretation. I. Title.
PA4037.V49   1985   883'.01   84–40672
ISBN 0–300–03339–7
ISBN 0–300–03395–8 (pbk.)

10   9   8   7   6   5   4   3   2   1

FOR VERA

CONTENTS

FOREWORD

"IT WOULD BE A PITY," SAID NIETZSCHE, "IF THE CLASSICS should speak to us less clearly because a million words stood in the way." His forebodings seem now to have been realized. A glance at the increasing girth of successive volumes of the standard journal of classical bibliography, *L'Année Philologique*, since World War II is enough to demonstrate the proliferation of writing on the subject in our time. Unfortunately, the vast majority of the studies listed will prove on inspection to be largely concerned with points of detail and composed by and for academic specialists in the field. Few are addressed to the literate but nonspecialist adult or to that equally important person, the intelligent but uninstructed beginning student; and of those few, very few indeed are the work of scholars of the first rank, equipped for their task not merely with raw classical erudition but also with style, taste, and literary judgment.

It is a strange situation. On one side stand the classical masters of Greece and Rome, those models of concision, elegance, and understanding of the human condition, who composed least of all for narrow technologists, most of all for the Common Reader (and, indeed, the Common Hearer). On the other side stands a sort of industrial complex, processing those masters into an annually growing output of technical articles and monographs. What is lacking, it seems, in our society as well as in our scholarship, is the kind of book that

was supplied for earlier generations by such men as Richard
Jebb and Gilbert Murray in the intervals of their more technical researches—the kind of book that directed the general
reader not to the pyramid of secondary literature piled over
the burial places of the classical writers but to the living faces
of the writers themselves, as perceived by a scholar-humanist
with a deep knowledge of, and love for, his subject. Not only
for the sake of the potential student of classics, but also for
the sake of the humanities as a whole, within and outside
academe, it seems that this gap in classical studies ought to
be filled. The Hermes series is a modest attempt to fill it.

We have sought men and women possessed of a rather
rare combination of qualities: a love for literature in other
languages, extending into modern times; a vision that extends
beyond academe to contemporary life itself; and above all an
ability to express themselves in clear, lively, and graceful English, without polysyllabic language or parochial jargon. For
the aim of the series requires that they should communicate
to nonspecialist readers, authoritatively and vividly, their personal sense of why a given classical author's writings have
excited people for centuries and why they can continue to do
so. Some are classical scholars by profession, some are not;
each has lived long with the classics, and especially with the
author about whom he or she writes in this series.

The first, middle, and last goal of the Hermes series is to
guide the general reader to a dialogue with the classical masters rather than to acquaint him or her with the present state
of scholarly research. Thus our volumes contain few or no
footnotes; even within the texts, references to secondary literature are kept to a minimum. At the end of each volume,
however, is a short bibliography that includes recommended
English translations, and selected literary criticism, as well as
historical and (when appropriate) biographical studies.

Throughout, all quotations from the Greek or Latin texts are given in English translation.

In these ways we hope to let the classics speak again, with a minimum of modern verbiage (as Nietzsche wished), to the widest possible audience of interested people.

John Herington

PREFACE

THE DISTINCTION OF HOMER'S POETRY LIES IN THE WAY THE story is presented as action continuously developing moment to moment, act after act. Hence the swift dramatization of the material, the immediate presentation of the characters, the visualization of events. The treatment is concrete. Objects are made tangible the moment they are brought to the forefront by the action. A vital movement informs the narrative. Indeed, we find in Homer not so much narrative as drama, or events in the making.

The following pages deal largely with the poetic quality intrinsic to this mode of representation. It is my aim to show how such poetry has a universal appeal for listeners or readers, how appreciation of it does not require any introduction to Homer's cultural milieu. Indeed, it is a distinctive quality of the Homeric poems that they are so self-contained, that their style is intrinsic to the way things are perceived, that they absorb the mythical background or silently exclude what is incompatible with their spirit.

How do we account for a treatment that lets the action flow so consistently on its own strength? What stands out is the sense of time: the specific focus on act after act, on moment after moment. Homer's hexameter is wonderfully adapted to bring out the lingering transience of these acts, these moments. My translations aim to convey this effect. They have no artistic claim, they are simply an attempt somehow to render the rhythm of Homeric verse. I have thus marked the principal caesura, or break, in the third foot which, by breaking the line in two parts, gives the sense of an upward and downward movement, thus suggesting the actual moment of time which, like breath, encompasses the lingering act.

It was of course impossible to reproduce the modulations of the Greek; but something could be done by letting each English half-verse have a rhythm of its own and yet merging the two halves into one greater tune. Where possible, I have marked the caesura after the corresponding English word. At times, since the word preceding the caesura bears a certain emphasis, I have repeated it in my translation: in such cases this appeared the best way to give the line its fullness.

Similar reasons may justify my hyphenations. Since the cadence of the verse is such as to hold in suspense any momentary act, the imagery finds its place in it by contributing an element of solidity or weight and letting the transient moment linger before it comes to a close. Hence my hyphenated noun-epithet phrases. They are intended to show that noun and epithet form one rhythmical unit of meaning, a balancing image, not a phrase to be analyzed in terms of a substantive qualified by its attributes. Thus, for instance, in the verse "and to him in reply / thus spoke swift-footed Achilles," the narrative meaning "Achilles replied" is given a natural suspense that finds its climax in the word *reply* and comes to a dying fall or a standstill in the solid "swift-footed Achilles." The initial pulse prompts an expectation which is fulfilled at the end. The rhythm itself suggests a sequence that is essential to life.

I HOMER AND
THE READER

I

The child's first impressions on hearing Homer are as deep as they are vivid. The wrath of Achilles conjured up all at once; Achilles and Agamemnon standing out in strife against each other; Chryses suddenly appearing before the Achaeans to ransom his daughter; Chryses rebuffed and walking in angry prayer along the shore; Apollo listening and descending from Olympus—such scenes, enacted as they are moment after moment, are naturally impressive by virtue of their own strength.

How to explain the spell they cast upon a child's mind? How to explain it quite apart from any preliminary learning? One reason for it is precisely that no preliminary learning is required. For these scenes are self-contained and self-explanatory. What they present comes to life through a power of its own. It is indeed the suddenness of realization which makes them so forcible.

Take the wrath of Achilles, the first thing mentioned in the *Iliad*. No need for any narrative detail. His wrath is immediately singled out because it is momentous, explosive by its very nature. Is it simply an overwhelming human emotion or, rather, a divine power? No matter. So bold and forthright is its presentation that it appears as an uncontroversial and central event in its own right, rising far above the incidental

occasion. We wonder, but hardly question. Even before we
learn the full story, this wrath inhabits our imagination. And
in this we are at one with the child. The apprehended thing
is as real as the apprehending mind is malleable, receptive,
elastic.

Or take the appearance of Chryses, the starting point of
the action in the *Iliad* (1.12ff.):

> he came to the Achaean swift ships
> to have his daughter released / and bearing an infinite
>   ransom,
> holding the crown in his hands / the crown of far-
>   shooting Apollo
> over the golden sceptre, / and to all the Achaeans he so
>   prayed

Again the power of the bold, forthright stroke. There are
no preliminaries. We are told nothing about the raid, the plun-
der, the occasion that saw a father bereft, a daughter dragged
away. All the more majestic does the old man's figure appear
against the silent background—as if the burden of experience
were simply understood in the compelling visual significance
of a suppliant human shape.

To appreciate this presentation more fully, let us give rein
to that naive capacity to visualize even while we read or listen.
For we touch here on something concrete and universally appealing, a plastic form in the expression. See, in this instance,
how the god's name with its epithet and the mention of the
divine emblems accrue to the man's presence, composing one
encompassing image. Solidly implanted, he suddenly stands
before us. Solidity and suddenness blend, giving the whole
scene a compact quality. Chryses is not described first and
dramatized later. No, the speech that follows is like an ema-
nation of his presence. He is all at one with his function here

and now; he hardly exists apart from what he does, says, and appears to be in the present instance. How could it be otherwise? you may ask. And yet this simplicity is the rarest thing. A poetic logic expunges all extraneous details, giving us the sense of an inevitable development.

The next moment sees Chryses withdrawing, rejected by Agamemnon:

> So he spoke. Suddenly feared / the old man and obeyed his word
> and in silence he walked / by the shore-of-the-wide-roaring-sea.
> Then, as he moved away, / intense was the old man's prayer
> to Apollo the king / whom-fair-tressed-Leto-gave-birth-to:
> "Listen, o Silver-bow. . . .

A solitary man walking along the shore absorbed in fateful prayer—a picture both simple and pregnant, such as to impress the child and give pause to the scholar. Why is this so? The reason again lies in sudden compact imagery grasped at one stroke. The sea-smitten shore conspires all at once with the presence of the man and his emotion. Even as we follow him, Chryses blends with the space which the brief and yet ample cadence of the verse summons up in the resounding name of the sea.

These initial remarks could be applied in various ways to many passages throughout the poems. What is this quality that lies at the core of Homer's art? It is the capacity to let a thing become an image the moment it is mentioned; and by "image" I mean a thing rendered so as to be strongly fixed in the field of vision, both a presence in itself and an element in the narrative sequence. In Homer, to mention is to summon up, to realize. Such an image clings to the perceptive mind of the reader or listener. It has a power of attraction; and any apposition immediately leans upon it, becomes part of it, holding in check any comment or digression.

Why is it, for instance, that Andromache is so impressive when she meets Hector in *Il.* 6.394ff.? One reason is her mere presence on the ramparts of Troy and, along with it, the way she is presented as an image:

> There the bountiful wife / came face to face running to meet him
> Andromache who was daughter / of Eetion-the-great-hearted
> Eetion who once lived / under mount Placus-rich-wooded
> in Hypoplacian Thebes / and on the Cilicians held sway;
> his own daughter it was / now wedded to Hector-bronze-armed;
> Hector there did she meet, / and with her was walking the handmaid
> holding the child on her bosom, / the tender child, but an infant,
> Hector's son the belovéd, / like to a beautiful star.

If we were to take the text literally or as mere narrative, we would hardly have any idea of how simple the means, how strong the effect. Andromache comes running, she is suddenly there; and verse after verse, her presence acquires substance through the names and epithets of father, city, country which, weighty as they are, still seem to quiver with the initial impact of her appearance. As if by a miracle, we have fullness of form without description. Any further detail would weaken the point of focus, within whose vital range the nurse and child take their place—no narrative addition, but extension of the same movement, as in the encompassing rhythm of a sculptural group.

Or take Priam coming to Achilles in *Il.* 24.477ff.:

> Unnoticed by them did he enter / great Priam, and standing close by
> he laid hold of Achilles; / clasped his knees, kissed his hands
> dreadful murderous hands / that had slain many of his sons.
> And as when deep folly / comes upon one that at home
> has taken the life of a man / and to other people he comes
> into a rich great house, / amazement besets those who see him;
> thus was Achilles amazed / at the sight of Priam-the-godlike
> and amazed were they all, / and at one another they looked.

The passage makes explicit what is everywhere implicit in the poet's art: sudden and outright visualization. Not without reason does Priam enter unseen, an immediate, amazing presence heightened by the simile. The reader's wonder thus becomes that of the bystanders who suddenly see him and gaze at one another. Surprise, contemplation, nothing portentous or spectacular; simply an old man's appearance surrounded by unfathomable silence.

We may compare a passage from the *Odyssey* 1.328ff.:

> Up from her chamber did she / in her heart catch the song god-inspired

she the daughter of Icarius, / Icarius' thoughtful
   Penelope;
and by the lofty stairs / down she came from her room
not alone but together / also two handmaids came with
   her.
Then when among the suitors / she arrived, the-divine-
   among-women,
she stood still by the pillar / the pillar of the-closely-
   built-roof,
over in front of her cheeks / holding up the glistening
   veil;
and with her, there, at each side / a careful handmaid
   stood by.
Then breaking out in tears / she spoke to the singer
   divine.

This is our first meeting with Penelope in the *Odyssey*. Again, there is no wearisome introduction: the person's identity merges with the appearance itself. She is presented on the spur of the moment, on the last note of Phemius's music, no sooner mentioned than standing before us. Whatever details are given are not descriptive but touches in her materialization; for her approach, her stance, her holding the veil are hardly things intended to satisfy our curiosity or our taste for realism. What we have here is something of a more fundamental nature. Each detail both builds up Penelope's image and advances the action. It is as if a progressive rhythm made her more and more palpable step by step. We have, in each instance, a moment that lingers in the suspense of the verse and does not pass without leaving a vital contour. What emerges is a growing sense of form. Even the handmaids on either side of her contribute to it, like figures at the extremities of a pediment.

Compare, in the same book (lines 102ff.), Athena's appearance in Ithaca:

> She went down from Olympus / down from its peaks
>   with a leap;
> she stood in Ithaca's land / right there at Odysseus's
>   portals,
> upon the courtyard's threshold: / and she held a spear
>   in her hand
> resembling a guest in looks, / even Mentes king of the
>   Taphians.

Again, the presentation is as simple as it is powerful: no account of Athena's flight from Olympus to Ithaca, no strange epiphany as she arrives, simply the purest motion and position. The Greek verbs have a striking effect. *To go, to leap, to stand*: it is as if the goddess were an instant embodiment of these acts, as if these simple acts acquire through her a portentous substance and quality. She thus naturally appears in human form, like Mentes, as she usually does when seen with Telemachus. Homer's anthropomorphism is true to his sense of form.

II

The image-making process continually tends to absorb the narrative. Thus the Penelope passage quoted above occurs elsewhere (cp. *Od.* 16.414ff., 18.206ff., 21.63ff.); so does the verse portraying Athena's leap (*Il.* 2.167, 4.74, etc.); and, with slight variations, the verse portraying a man walking, like Chryses, by the sea (cp. *Il.* 1.327, 9.182, *Od.* 4.432). The narrative hardly affects these image-making positions or movements; on the contrary, it is the narrative (or the ebb and flow of circumstance) which is magnetically drawn around them.

Least of all can the Homeric poems be read with a vo-

racious interest in plot and its dénouement. It is not so much
a question of reading as of rereading, absorbing, becoming
attuned. The reader may even find the literal content disap-
pointing; but what will challenge his imagination, if he is at
all sensitive, is the representation itself. For sheer variety of
incidents or for fantastic and mythical events, he will turn
with advantage elsewhere: here, the poetry lies in a fundamental way of being, of happening.

A way of being, of happening: this is what Homer's recurring imagery is all about. Why is it that by its recurrence
it does not dull our senses but, rather, never ceases to delight
us? How is it that Homer's poetry, qua poetry, is hardly con-
ceivable without it? We here come to a crux of modern scholarship, its tantalizing effort to justify Homer's so-called
formulas (or repeated phrases and sentences), which it re-
gards as a Homeric peculiarity alien to modern taste and only
to be appreciated as a form of "oral" compositional technique.
What lies in question here is Homer's style. We must do justice to it. We must try to see how it is, not only *not* alien to
modern taste, but how it satisfies that primordial instict for
form which is common to all poetry.

The response of the common reader, or even of the child,
may be of interest to the critic on this point. How often we
come across people who have a vague knowledge or memory
of Homer but still remember with pleasure such phrases as
"swift-footed Achilles," "rose-fingered Dawn," "resounding
sea," "wingéd words," "long-shadowed spear." Why? These
phrases are in themselves memorable, haunting. And yet the
reader would soon forget them did they not often recur in the
poems, and at significant vantage-points. For they are not
mannerisms or mere figures of speech: they arrest the transient image where verse and sense allow it, lifting it above
the blunting literal meaning of the surrounding passage. The

realization of images is thus generalized into a typical mode of expression. Form emerges, as it were, from below—from a sense of sheer existence surfacing above the shifting relations of the narrative.

Consider the simplest designation of things. In *Il.* 3.346–47, for instance: "First did Alexander send forth the long-shadowed-spear and he struck on Menelaus' all-even-shield." Spear and shield are given in Homeric form: their recurring shape makes them at once familiar and impressive. But no less recurrent is that "sending forth" and that "striking" of metal against metal. The epithets thus give sensuous evidence and weight to the moment; and such a moment so binds the thing to its intrinsic occasion that the narrative interest wanes and we might even forget who is striking whom, seeing nothing but the actuality of the event arrested in its form.

Compare "sailing with the well-benched ship over the wine-colored sea" (*Il.* 7.88), "we came with the dark, swift ship" (*Od.* 3.61), and "They steered the ships-that-are-curved-on-both-sides" (10.91). Would not the simple verb *to sail* do as well? Why is this sailing so richly expressed? The reason is that it is not taken for granted. Wherever an opening perspective allows it, we are made to see the ship image itself, a shape against the background of the sea.

The same applies to people. Why, for instance, "swift-footed Achilles so spoke"? Why an epithet for any hero speaking, rising, standing, or moving? Again, it is a question of sudden relief. The fleeting human occasion brings the hero's image to the forefront. How effective in this connection is the epithet "swift-footed"! The very fact that it has no pointed connection to anything else makes Achilles' image clear and strong in itself and by itself, utterly absorbed into the position and stance of the moment.

The reader of Homer can easily multiply such instances.

Everything in the poems flashes brightly before it passes away; and yet everything also finds its place and moment by striving toward constant outline and rhythm. Occurrences become recurrences; and, through persisting association, the things so brought into play acquire an intrinsic function, take position and form, become as symbolic of themselves as they are true to nature. Here is a self-consistent fullness upon the strength of which anything mentioned tends to appear as an inevitable image.

For the poet's treatment is never fastidiously graphic, realistic, minute. From the tangled mass of things and their occasions what stands out is anything that has contour or resonance. Thus the forward movement of a warrior conjures up that of a lion; his fall, that of a tree cut down by the foresters. Why is it that the similes strike up analogies to the human action throughout the world of nature? Not, certainly, for mere ornament or to provide a break in tense passages. Rather, the image-making force breaks through the bounds of a passage and gathers its own force, drawing the poetry toward a sense of form and away from narrative or description.

The world is thus both simplified and enriched with life—reduced, that is to say, to vantage-grounds that are scenes of action: windy Troy no less than rocky Ithaca. And this concentration is no less true of any focal point on Homer's large canvas—no less true of a throbbing heart than it is of sea-smitten shore. Hardly anything is mentioned that is not singled out and sharply exposed insofar as it crystallizes an act or a state of being. We have at one and the same time an object and a pulse of life.

It is no wonder, then, that Homer's image-making sentences have a haunting effect, that even the casual reader remembers them over and above the specific subject matter. It is not really a question of vivid coloring. The reason goes much deeper. We touch, rather, upon ontological grounds. To read here is to tap the imaginative source of our understanding, to carry out in the realm of art that process which we have also carried out in actual life before our perceptions were jaded into notions taken for granted. "What is that?" asks a child, pointing to a train or a waterfall; and there is a vital urge to know in the question, a vital realization in the answer. He now recognizes things. They appear to him in the fresh evidence of their existence, taking their pertinent place in the field of vision. A word becomes a discovery. Rather than a display of fluid impressions, here form arises in all its aesthetic cogency, with delight in its definition, with wonder at its significance. And the spell persists until it is lost in a hackneyed order of things learned by rote. What then? Lost forever? No. Poetry—and art in general—come to remove, as Coleridge puts it, the "film of familiarity which blinds us to the truth and wonder of the world about us."

This poetic effect is eminently Homeric. A fresh sense of life and resilience is always brought home to us by letting the image of a thing come into view on the cadence of a verse that does no more than realize in rhythm a basic movement or position. The music and the imagery blend with the vocabulary. It is as if a new poetic language came into our ken. Here the "long-shadowed spear" finds its place as well as the "wing-stretching birds" or the "robe-trailing women" or the "taper-leaved olive-tree"—each thing singled out in its individuality and yet bearing the mark of a common touch.

This delight in images is increased by their recurrences and the kindred patterns of form they cast over existence. What ultimately comes into play is a sense of recognition, a primal urge to establish identities, what metaphysicians call "the principle of individuation." For nothing is dearer to the mind than to perceive, and perceive clearly, a faculty which

Homer's imagery elicits on a large scale. The interest of finding the same Homeric phrase over and over again is no idle
pleasure. We look for resemblances in whatever we see. It
means finding our way through the multiplicity of things.

We undergo the same process on a more elementary level
when we first learn our native language: words are deeply
assimilated in that they seem to conspire with the order of
nature. Homer leads us to abridge and intensify this process.
His imagery gives us essential contours of the things or phenomena which we actually see in the world around us; and
the recurrences of his image-making phrases suggest corresponding harmonies in existence itself. For Homer avoids
what is merely peculiar, something that could be remembered
only so long as the interest in it remains. Nothing is here
merely "interesting." The apprehension of a shape, distinctive as it is, suggests an encompassing sense of form; and this
sense of form evokes kindred objects the world over. Curiosities could not be so suggestive. If Homer's imagery deeply
affects the reader, the reason is that it is solidly implanted in
the perception of nature.

III

Modern scholarship has deterred the reader from taking
Homer's expression at its face value. Between the poet and
nature it has interposed the thick wall of what is called tradition or "traditional poetry": formulas, themes, conventions,
and techniques that are usually taken for granted.

We must encourage the frightened reader to think for
himself, to appreciate Homeric poetry by appealing directly
to the truth of nature. Or, conversely, we may look at nature
through Homeric eyes. For the poet's meaning must be given
its full force. It does not merely consist in the designation of
a literal fact or a statement that can be stripped of stylistic

superfluities. The wording itself is most important. It implies a whole mode of perception and expression.

Indeed many of the "formulas" are most significant in this respect, particularly those recurring verses which arrest an event in the moment of its image-making realization. For example,

    Il. 1.476, etc.

> When the early-born one appeared / Dawn-with-her-
>   fingers-of-rose

spells out the moment when the slanting rays of the rising sun actually *touch* into radiance anything exposed to their light. Those fingers express contact, that rose is sensuous freshness as well as color. Do we have here a goddess or simply a natural phenomenon? Both at the same time. The image contains the sense of what is occurring. Hence the felicity of the expression.

    Od. 2.388, etc.

> Then did the sun sink down / and enshadowed were all
>   the streets

may remind us of Virgil's *maioresque cadunt altis de montibus umbrae*, "and longer the shadows fall down from the heights of the mountains." But Homer's verse is simpler and universally applicable, rendering no picturesque effect but evoking that imponderable moment when, in any place, things lose their edge as day yields to night.

    Od. 13.79, cp. 2.398, etc.

> Upon him did sleep / sweet sleep on the eye-lids fall

makes the moment palpable; for we realize the truth of experience at a most sensitive point, that soft pressure which "weighs the eye-lids down" (cp. Shakespeare, *Henry IV*, part 2, 3.1.6).

> *Od.* 4.794, 18.189

> There she sank back in sleep, / and all her joints were set loose

conveys the actual breathing-space between waking and sleep, the sweet abandon of a woman's body (cp. *Od.* 20.57, *Il.* 23.62).

> *Il.* 17.695–96, etc.

> Long was silence upon him, / wordless; the eyes
> with tears were filled, / and checked was the
>   flourishing voice.

Here is no cry, no gesture, no realistic touch fitted to the particular occasion. This silence is more eloquent, more broadly significant: we all know the moment of amazement or grief that defies all words.

> *Il* 1.201, etc.

> And at once speaking out / he addressed to her wingéd words.

The truth of this verse is borne home to us when our words come spontaneously, prompted suddenly by the passing occasion, taking flight.

> *Od.* 9.67–69, cp. 5.292–94, 12.313–15

> A wind he stirred, the North-wind, / Zeus-assembler-
>   of-clouds
> with wondrous blast, / and with fog did he encompass
> the earth at once and the sea, / down from the sky
>   emerged night.

Further description would weaken the meaning. We know the

sudden impact of a storm: a turning-point or a single touch
all at once encompassing the elements. The god thus has a
poetic function, bringing the various phenomena within the
compass of the same power, so that any detailed account is
left out of the picture.

Il. 1.481–82, *Od.* 2.427–28

Full blew the wind, / mid-sail, and the wave
round the bows darkly-seething / sang loud, as the ship
    moved on.

Wind, sail, wave, sound make one instant vital impression.
A boat passing with swelling sails will ever give us such an
airy, joyous sense of movement.

What do all these instances have in common? If they
induce us to look at things with Homeric eyes, in what way
do they summon up an image of reality?

In the first place, they do not describe in detail, they do
not explain, but let the object of representation simply be what
it is before it passes away. We have an outline as clear as it is
swift, no arbitrary development, emphasis, no exaggeration.
Further, they do not merely report a happening, they do not
merely mention a thing. Whatever is said must be given its
rightful cadence, its proper ground and moment. Hence no
flimsiness, but a natural fullness of representation.

In other words, and to put the matter positively, what we
have is concrete realization. This means that an event is seen
in its actuality: the doing, the taking place, the coming to
fruition are implicit in the expression, quite apart from any
narrative requirement. Thus "to utter wingéd words" is not
the same as "to say": the very phrase makes us feel the actual
achievement of the utterance—how a word suddenly exists,
how it finds its moment to fly out to the hearer. If, on the

other hand, I were to say, "the occasion immediately elicited these words from his lips," I would be explaining the situation and thus would lose the gracious moment of utterance. In the same way we may appreciate such phrases as "sleep fell on the eyelids" or "the rose-fingered Dawn appeared." Though they avoid any description of sleepiness or of early morning, they are not the same as "he fell asleep" or "it was day-break." What we always find is an immediate sense of the occurrence itself—how it materializes, how it is verified instantly at a fine point of contact.

Things find here an intrinsic function that brings them to the fore; and, by the same token, functions appear unthinkable without a thing to give them body. Hence the vitality of this imagery. The "formulas" are no more than an ultimate flagrant example of Homeric concreteness. Strip any event of all accessories, strip it of all descriptive and casual details, yet maintain a sense of its emergence in the field of vision—what remains? Nothing but simplicity and fullness of outline. So in Homer, we find the constant striving toward form: in the battle scenes, for instance, the relentless clash and clang and fall; in the animal similes, the perpetual attack, pursuit, escape.

But why is this form so forceful? Because it never degenerates into stale mannerism, because it vibrates with life. We have here a poetic measure that pervades the language. Quite apart from any particular imagery, it is found in the simplest instances. Any act or state appears reduced to the essentials of position and movement, and yet it is filled with its own intrinsic force. We are not told, as we are in an ordinary or easy-going narrative, that a man goes or stops somewhere: no, his going is presented as if it were a movement taking a body; his standing, as if it were a body finding its moment of rest, resistance, balance. The same effect is achieved in rendering, say, a wave or a rock. A thing always blends with the significance of its concrete position to which the surrounding action gives a dramatic relevance. The resulting image seems to be produced by the movement stilled within it or by the weight that holds it where it is.

The mere fact of standing or moving thus seems to have its own solemnity, so intimately is it fused with a body. "Who is that broad strong man conspicous among the Argives, rising above them by his head and large shoulders?" Priam asks Helen (*Il.* 3.226ff.), and she replies, "That is Ajax-the-massive-one, wall to the Achaeans; and Idomeneus, like a god in the midst of the Cretans, stands out beyond; and around him the chiefs of the Cretans are gathered." Compare Odysseus's rendering of Ithaca (*Od.* 9.21): "Ithaca-seen-from-afar do I inhabit; in it a mountain, leaf-shaking Neritos, clear to the eye; and many islands around stand out very near one another, Dulichium and Same and wooded Zacynthus." The expressions are both plain and strong. The reason lies in the sharp sense of position, the sheer wonder of a body seen standing where it is, no matter whether it is the body of an island or a person (note that the verb *naietaō*, "to inhabit," applies both to people and to places: places inhabit the earth just as people inhabit places). As a result, what we might take for granted is felt in its existential value. The islands, as well as the heroes, take position, form a constellation, creating their own space and opening up an airy perspective.

In the same light consider a simile (*Il.* 5.522ff.): "They stood like clouds which Zeus sets still upon the peaks of mountains in the windless air—steadfast as long as the Northwind is asleep." Again here is a strong sense of position. It gives life to the simile. That precarious stillness imparts to such disparate things as clouds and men an instant relevance;

their shapes are rendered as being at one with a point of balance or a poise in existence. The similes seem to grow out of the very way the poet looks at the world.

Image-making moments whose truth is the ultimate reason both for their literal recurrences and for the broader analogies which they persistently suggest, moments as real in themselves as they are typical of what must inevitably happen or exist—these produce a mode of expression that is embedded in Homer's style. The style itself is thus part and parcel of the Homeric imagination; for it naturally brings out basic patterns in the flux of existence and, in so doing, is at one with Homer's tendency to humanize or naturalize whatever the subject matter affords. The reader who is seeking extraordinary things will be disappointed to find Homer restrained in this respect—disappointed, for instance, at the fact that Achilles in Homer is not at all invulnerable, not at all a portentous being. How could he be when he, as inevitably as anyone else, must launch his long-shadowed spear, must nimbly ply his feet and knees, must feel his heart sway with passion, must be shown as a recumbent figure crushed with grief?

II THE STORY

I

It was the genius of Homer to center his poetry on a single action, thought Aristotle. "Homer carries away the listener into the midst of events as if they were known already," sang Horace. These judgments are rightly famous. But how can we explain this directness, this plunge to the heart of the matter, the fact that Homer chose to focus on one action rather than a cycle of myths or the Trojan War or one hero's life as a whole? Whence came this clarity of focus that makes the Homeric poems so different from other epics, and indeed from any large-scale narrative?

One reason lies in the sudden realization of images I mentioned in the previous chapter. We are immediately brought face to face with the characters as they stand forth and play their part. We find representation rather than narration, hence an action unfolding from moment to moment rather than a story *about* events. It is as if the style fashioned the story. Those Homeric sentences which let each act linger at its proper place and moment could hardly apply to an epic embracing indefinite periods of time or to a plot whose complications presupposed an elaborate background and facts not openly enacted.

It follows that the plots of both poems are very simple. That of the *Iliad* may be summarized as follows.

Agamemnon refuses his captive Chryseis to her father,

Chryses, priest of Apollo; the god, in response to Chryses' prayers, sends a plague upon the army. Spurred by Achilles, the seer Chalcas reveals the reason for the plague, at which point Agamemnon yields Chryseis but seizes Achilles' Briseis. Achilles' wrath flares up. He will fight no more; he is proof against all entreaty. As a result, the Achaeans are defeated; to save them, Achilles sends in his beloved friend, Patroclus, who is slain by the Trojan Hector. Grief now replaces wrath in Achilles. To avenge his friend, he in turn slays Hector. Widespread grief reigns in Troy. Hector's father, Priam, comes to Achilles to ransom his son's corpse. The two men weep over their respective dead. The poem ends with Hector's funeral.

And the plot of the *Odyssey*:

In Ithaca, Odysseus is still being missed twenty years after he sailed for Troy, while a band of suitors woos his wife, Penelope. Their son, Telemachus, now of age, is stirred by Athena to go and seek his father. In the meantime, Odysseus is in Calypso's island, Ogygia, having been shipwrecked there seven years earlier, and is now the nymph's unwilling lover, longing for home. But the same moment of urgency strikes here as it does in Ithaca. The nymph, at the behest of Zeus, lets Odysseus go. On a raft he builds himself, he reaches the Phaeacians, to whom he recounts his wanderings; they convey him back to Ithaca. His landing coincides with the return of Telemachus from his quest. A plot is laid against the suitors, who are killed. Odysseus and Penelope are reunited and the islanders appeased.

Here is simplicity and a sense of inevitability in the outline. The plot is such that the reader may divine its development right from the beginning. And this is not because the story is known in advance or because the gods so decide—at least not primarily so. It is, rather, because of a quality intrinsic to the art itself, because of the way the characters are shown assuming their basic roles, as if prophetic of their fate.

Take Achilles. He must have loomed large in the poet's mind even before the composition of the poem, visualized as an image powerfully present yet setting in motion the course of ensuing events. "Not because of the Trojan spearmen I came hither to fight; for in no way are they guilty to me" (*Il.* 1.152ff.), he cries out to Agamemnon; and in so saying he also foreshadows his withdrawal from the war. "By this staff I swear. . . . a desire for Achilles will come one day to the sons of the Achaeans" (1.233ff.); and his oath portends the imminent rout of the Achaeans. "Ah, my child, why did I rear you and give you so dreadful a birth? Would that by the ships you could sit without pain, without tears" (1.414ff.), his mother exclaims to him soon after; and her words surely suggest the imminent death of Patroclus as well as Achilles' own doom. Hector is no different: "Your bravery will kill you," Andromache tells him in the earlier part of the poem (6.407), and her handmaids mourn for him as if he were already dead, thus foreshadowing the poem's end. There is no oracle, no avowed decree of fate that predetermines the career of these heroes; or, at least, this is not emphasized. What drives them to their destiny are the positions they immediately take. Their presence summons up the action, which, in turn, draws them to its inevitable conclusion.

And look at Odysseus. Time and again he is presented in incisive and deepening outline as a dweller on Calypso's island, surfeited with her love, yearning for home, scanning the boundless sea through his tears (*Od.* 1.13–15, 57–62; 5.13–15, 151–58); and his image is a haunting one—central, magnetic, stirring the interest of the gods, naturally portending the day of return. Nor is his plight narratively connected with

affairs in Ithaca. What motivates the action is, again, his image—dim at first in Telemachus' mind and then growing into
compelling clarity through Athena's inspiration. A similar
process occurs in the account of his wanderings. What persistently stands out is a man with his crew, landing, seeking
his bearings, finding a refuge or an escape, sailing onward in
grief for lost friends; and we have not so much a tale of adventures or travels as a series of instances in which the variety
of circumstances is just a foil to the man's presence. Even in
the latter part of the *Odyssey*, where the plot thickens, the
disguised Odysseus is a figure constantly suggestive of who
he actually is and what he might be in other lands—sometimes inscrutable and sometimes transparent almost to the
point of recognition, elusive and yet pervasive, naturally
swaying the action one way then the other as, step by step,
his influence or prestige grows clearer and at last his full
identity stands revealed. Again the story is seen in terms of
a self-revealing image.

Crucial moments thus arrest a hero's image and condition
the plot rather than being conditioned by it: Achilles in his
wrath, Achilles in his grief, Achilles in his revenge, Achilles
in his final human awareness; or Odysseus yearning for
home, Odysseus being missed, Odysseus wandering, Odysseus returning. Much of Homer's power is due to this integration of the action with a character's image. There is no
need to recall or explain the connections. These heroes hardly
ever speak to draw the plot together but, rather, to account
for their sheer presence. Position, contiguity, and sequence
are enough to reflect the silent logic of things or of fate, as in
the scenes of a bas-relief whose figures are simultaneously
self-explanatory and suggestive of events that reverberate far
beyond them.

II

If the plot is so simple, dependent on a single action whose dramatic movement excludes any long detailed narrative or description, what is it that accounts for the large scale of the poems?

The answer lies in the way events are conceived. A sudden occasion presents a hero at one with his action; and the imaginative impact is such as to summon up a whole tract of concomitant experience, precipitating further occasions of a similar kind. Action, in other words, is seen in its voluminous context. For just as one incident, though naturally unique, is still one of many, so it naturally suggests its likeness. It diffuses. The movement that brings it about is pervasive, producing the same effect here and there, near and far. We are made to feel how occurrences are both singular and typical.

What comes to the fore is thus one massive action so condensed and presented as inevitable in the interplay of its single instances that we hardly ask why it happened to come about as it did, as we do in history or in novels. Here is the way things happen rather than facts construed so as to lead to one another. Hence a specious, swelling present—the Homeric day expanding over the field of vision, engrossed in the recurring beat of the action. What we normally see in terms of cause and effect is here presented in terms of contiguity. Justifications and imputations tend to be set aside; things speak for themselves. Events thus find their reason in the very fact of being parallel or successive, as if their emergence were due to existential necessity rather than to any arbitrary plot.

And yet there is convergence. The general trend is all encompassing—call it fate, nature, or the will of the gods. What ultimately justifies any occurrence in the poems is, if nothing else, the irony of things; and from this perspective, anything may find its place there, as long as it is clearly perceived and solid enough to share the weight of the expanding moment.

Thus the battle scenes of the *Iliad* from book 4 to book 17 are far more extensive than might be required by the plot of bringing about the Achaean defeat, the death of Patroclus, and the return of Achilles. Their tenuous relation to the plot becomes negligible. What matters is a pregnant juxtaposition: on the one hand, the continuing struggle of the war and, on the other, Achilles aloof, brooding, enclosed in his wrath. So, quite apart from the hero's withdrawal, the poet shows us the ebb and flow of the fighting, the man-to-man encounter in and by itself. There is one great crisis, one stroke of fate in its separate manifestations. As in the large composition of a painting, things take their distance from the central theme and yet are so rendered as to participate in it, even unwittingly.

Therefore the battle scenes, for all their extension, in no way complicate the plot. On the contrary, they stress its stark simplicity. "First Antilochus slew a Trojan spearman brave among the foremost, Ekhepolus son of Thalysius; him he first struck on the horn of the horse-crested helmet, through the forehead pieced the brazen point . . . darkness covered his eyes, like a tower he fell in the strong combat" (4.457ff.). And then (4.473ff.): "There Telamonian Ajax struck the son of Anthemius, Simoeisius the flourishing youth. . . . through the shoulder went the brazen spear; to the ground he fell like a poplar." Time and again we see the occurrence itself—the clash, the fall. Time and again a universal theme is rehearsed in the same essential outlines: young life laid low, darkness covering the eyes, limbs unstrung. The similes comparing a hero's fall to that of a tree (13.178, 389; 14.414; 16.482; 17.53,

etc.) or the human clash to the attack of animal upon animal
(8.338; 11.113, 172; 12.41; 13.471, etc.) remove us even further
from the plot or any topical interest. We witness, rather, an
existential condition affecting the whole world. The doom of
battles and the doom of such emotions as the wrath of Achilles
exist in their own right, in whatever way they may produce
each other or be assigned to any particular cause. Through
this massive juxtaposition the story broadens immeasurably
while remaining what it is.

The same reasoning may be applied to the *Odyssey*. Again
we find one central event as brief as it is voluminously rendered through the occasions which, from separate places,
concur to build it up. For the moment of Odysseus' return is
all-pervasive. It strikes on Olympus where Athena has no
other thought. It strikes in Ogygia where Calypso must let
Odysseus go. It strikes in Ithaca, where it bestirs Telemachus
to his quest for his father. And no other concern appears more
urgent in Pylus and Sparta when Telemachus visits them.
Even the tale of Odysseus' wanderings takes its relative place
in this expanding movement: continually merging with his
own image, is it not a way of revealing himself to the Phaeacians who take him home? Odysseus must appear as what he
really is on the eve of his return.

As in the *Iliad*, the simplicity of the plot thus goes hand
in hand with the large scale of the composition. For the long
days that comprise Odysseus' return also bring into evidence
a whole stretch of existence in different places, highlighting
what is relevant not so much to the plot as to life itself. It is
so in Pylus, Sparta, Phaeacia—and it is so in Ithaca. Even
while Odysseus looms ahead or is actually present, we see
not only the main characters in their steadfast roles but the
minstrel singing, the banquets in full array, the sacrifices, libations, and omens. The same daylight shines on each and

all; it starts off the spectacle of life, sanctioning the rightness of each daily act and leaving the innocence of things unimpaired. It is as though even the tensest action, down to its bloody denouement, could only run its course through the bounties of existence, through what gives life its immanent glow. Thus doom closes in upon the feasting, banqueting suitors. Odysseus' arrow strikes Antinous just as he is lifting the wine-cup to his lips. "Who would think that at a banquet one man alone among many, even were he very strong, should bring him evil death and black doom?" asks the poet in a very rare instance of comment upon the action (*Od.* 22.12ff.).

III

Simplicity yet volume, unity of action yet a constant sense of the surrounding world—how is it that this simplicity so maintains its richness, and this volume so maintains its transparency? Why are we not wearied by either flimsiness or inert weight?

The reason lies in the way the representation of things is inextricably bound up with that of the action itself; for the action develops from moment to moment and as it takes place absorbs the reality of whatever it touches: what lies in its way comes naturally into view through the act that brings it to the fore, not through any separate description.

Look again at the beginning of the *Iliad*, the point at which Chryses withdraws praying and Apollo responds (1.34ff.):

And in silence he walked / by the shore-of-the-wide-
    roaring-sea;
then, as he moved away, / intense was the old man's
    prayer

to Apollo the king / whom-fair-tressed-Leto-gave-birth-
to:

"Listen, o Silver-bow, / you who stand over Chrysa
and over Cilla-the-sacred / and on Tenedos also have
sway,
Smintheus, if ever for you / a lovely shrine have I
roofed,
if indeed ever for you / fat thighs I, offering, burned
of bulls and of goats, if so / this my prayer now fulfill:
may the Danaans atone / for my tears by dint of your
shafts."

So did he speak in prayer, / and him heard Phoebus
Apollo,
and he came from Olympus, / down its peaks, full of
anger,
carrying the bow on his shoulders / and with it the
tightly-closed-quiver.
And a clang was made by the arrows / on the shoulder
of the god as he raged,
on his figure starting to move; / and he went in the
likeness of night.
He sat thereafter aloof / from the ships, and let go the
dart.
Dread was the clang which arose / up from the silver
bow.
On the mules it was first / he turned and on the swift
hounds,
then upon them themselves / aiming the sharp-piercing
shaft
he struck, and ever the pyres / thick burnt away with
the dead.
Nine days over the host / went off the shafts of the
god;

but on the tenth to the assembly / Achilles summoned
the people;
for in his mind did she put it, / the goddess Hera-
white-armed.
She took pity on the Trojans / in that she saw them
there dying.
And when they all had assembled / in one body
gathered together,
to them, then, standing up / so spoke swift-footed
Achilles. . . .

See how nothing is mentioned that is not immediately integrated into the upbeat and downbeat movement of each succeeding act: the seashore insofar as Chryses walks there; the
neighboring towns insofar as Apollo holds sway over them;
the prayer insofar as it is heard by the god, and the god insofar
as he hears it; the ridges of Olympus insofar as he treads upon
them; mules and dogs insofar as they are randomly hit;
Achilles insofar as he calls the assembly; Hera insofar as she
inspires him. In other words, nothing is introduced by way
of separate description or comment. Rather, each thing
emerges out of a quickening instant, everything concurs with
the expanding moment. The epithets, where they occur, only
mark highlights in the process. And yet, even while the action
drives us on, we almost unwittingly learn a great deal: here
is the relation between a priest and his god or between a
man's decision and divine inspiration. It is no less so with
the surrounding world: sea and mountain, the ships, the
nearby towns, the camp, the animals—all gradually compose
the picture. The narrative and its setting seem distilled into
experienced time, drop by drop.

Or consider, at the beginning of the *Odyssey,* the point at
which Athena is welcomed by Telemachus at Ithaca (1.125ff.):

Thus he spoke and he led her, / she followed him,
    Pallas Athena.
And when they were within / into the high-rising hall,
he took from her the spear, / stood it against the tall
    pillar,
into the spearstand, / the well-polished spearstand
    wherein
more spears of Odysseus-the-enduring / were standing
    up in great number.
Herself he led to a chair, / spreading a cloth as she sat,
to a beautiful high wrought chair, / with a stool below
    for her feet.
He drew up for himself a couch, / many-colored, away
    from the rest,
away from the suitors, in fear / that the guest be vexed
    by the noise
and be loath at the meal, / in the midst of the arrogant
    throng,
and so that about his father / his long-gone father he
    might ask.
Water then did a handmaid / bring up and pour from a
    bowl,
from a beautiful golden bowl / into a basin of silver
for washing the hands, by the side / a polished table
    she laid.

Act after act again brings each object to light. Each act
finds its point of contact, each thing its moment of focus. Here
again there is no separate description, no stale account of the
hall or its furniture and the meal. The spectacle of life inextricably blends with that of things. Table and chair, bowl and
basin, with their splendid epithets, confer a passing glow
upon what is happening.

This passage of the *Odyssey* is a familiar one. The welcoming of a guest is frequent throughout the poem. Some of the verses occur elsewhere with the same words (cp. *Od.* 4.52ff., 7.172ff., 17.91ff.). We have a typical scene which, by very virtue of being typical, may attune us to the way Homer tells his story. Is an important duel about to take place? Here is an arming scene, each item coming into full display the moment it is touched. Or a battle? We seldom find a general description, but the actual encounter of individuals: the clash, the blow, the fall. A departure or arrival? We are always given an instant glimpse of a vantage point the moment it is reached or left behind. And why is it that we cannot assemble a complete picture of a Homeric palace or Homeric armor though the poems deal with them so extensively? The reason is that Homer does not go out of his way to describe these things, but admits any relevant detail the moment it is brought to view by the passing act: "he crossed the brazen threshold," "they rested the chariot against the shining wall," "down she came from the upper chamber," "up through the eaves flew the bird," "through the belt and corslet drove the sharp arrow." Similarly, we find no general description of body or character (not even a general term for their designation), but a heart that prompts, a foot that moves, a hand that clasps.

IV

It follows that, in the poems, the action is solemn as well as it is simple. Acts which so instantly bring into play the basic features of whatever they touch are themselves basic— to come, to go, to take, to hold. Singled out as they are, and presented in rhythmical sequence, they seem to occur in their own right and take their place in the nature of things. They have their way of happening as surely as the break of day or the fall of night.

There is a natural solemnity in this. It lies in the fact that even the most ordinary acts are set in relief insofar as they are essential to life and inevitably mark a point in the course of the day. The plot is never allowed to obstruct this respect for the order of existence. The temperature may rise and things come to a head, but the basic pulse of time remains what it is: people rise from their sleep, get dressed, go out to face the day. Far from impending the main action, these ordinary acts root it in the ways of life.

Consider, in *Od.* 2.1ff., the point at which Telemachus starts out to challenge the suitors:

> When the early-born-one appeared / Dawn-with-the-fingers-of-rose,
> he sprang up from the bed / the dear son of Odysseus,
> and having donned his clothes / the sharp sword he slung round the shoulder,
> and under his glistening feet / he bound the beautiful sandals.
> He stepped out of his chamber, / like a god's was his presence,
> and at once on the heralds / the shrill-voiced heralds he called
> into the assembly to summon / the Achaeans-of-long-waving-hair.
> The heralds gave out the summons / and with great speed they were gathered
> And when they all had assembled / in one body gathered together,
> out he stepped to the assembly, / and held a bronze spear in his hand
> not alone, for together / two swift-footed hounds came out with him.

And divine was the beauty / shed on him by Pallas
    Athena;
while he was walking, the people / all looked upon him
    and wondered.
He then took his father's seat, / the elders yielded him
    place.

We are here witnessing a high point in Telemachus's life. For
the first time he is going to address the people of Ithaca, and
what prompts him is a matter of the greatest importance. We
might thus expect some account of his anxiety or of popular
feeling around him. But no, this day is like any other day. We
linger, rather, on each essential moment. All that matters, for
a while, are these ordinary proceedings. Given as they are in
a fixed form that recurs elsewhere (cp. *Od.* 4.306, 20.124, etc.),
they are what they are in themselves and by themselves, quite
apart from Telemachus's particular predicament. No other
narrative could be so oblivious of the plot while focusing on
the regular rhythms of life.

The general effect is one of calm and, at the same time,
dramatic development. These regularities of life are in no way
obtrusive. They give us the existential conditions of any action, however grave it may be. Thus the rising day bestirs
Telemachus; as it grows, it attends upon his acts; or, vice
versa, his acts are but the human counterpoint to the day's
progress. What else could Telemachus do at the moment?
What he does seems as inevitable as minute following minute.
Even so we walk, as we always must, to the edge of a preci-
pice; and so Telemachus takes the day in his stride, while
advancing toward a crucial act. Later, when he actually chal-
lenges the suitors, the denouement itself will appear to be an
inevitable outburst rather than a premeditated outcome of the
plot. The narrative is resolved into pulses of life.

Such a treatment requires condensation. Any complete account of the day's duration would of course be unthinkable, unless one were to attempt something like James Joyce's *Ulysses*. No, we only have essential moments. The story consists in a representation of reality witnessed step by step, but the treatment is not realistic. It would be quite unlike Homer to describe, for instance, Telemachus' moods and behavior; that would demand abstract observations, whereas Homer visualizes things the moment they happen. Nor, for the same reason, do we find any casual or random act: it would fail to give the passing moment its regular weight and cadence; we should be titillated rather than absorbed in the sheer occurrence.

Actions so outlined in their basic fullness naturally tend to exclude anything mean or vulgar. But, by the same token, anything extraordinary tends to be naturalized and made consistent with the flow of the human action. Thus, in the above passage, Athena's influence is subject to the occasion rather than the other way round. Though the plot might make her the agent of all that happens, it is not so in the actuality of what we see. The beauty she sheds upon Telemachus is one with the climax of his ripening youth as he steps out into his moment of glory. It is no metamorphosis. It has no practical effect. The people may wonder at him; but they are not shocked; and, after hearing him, they are silent, unable to help him by checking the encroaching suitors. What is the reason, then, for Athena's spell? It would not have been Homer's way to *describe* Telemachus. The quality of beauty itself had to be caught in its moment of realization; it is thus rendered as the effect of a divine touch.

Moments of life thus absorb the narrative, imposing upon it their own measure. These are Homeric moments. They are typical in that they remove us from any peculiarities of descriptive detail; they are concrete in that they present something actually taking place before our eyes. We see Telemachus rising, going out, confronting the people; and much as these acts are relevant to the topic at hand, still they have their own independent self-consistency and reality. Hence they give us a strong sense both of the present and of the permanent, of individual resilience and of general existence. Here is the rising occasion, and yet it is one with the recurring, self-renewing exertion of life. Telemachus presents himself with the freshness of morning. He does what we expect him to do, yet there is buoyancy in his step. This is how sunrise and sunset naturally come at the appointed times, without tiring us. The poetic touch lies in bringing out the wonder of what is familiar.

V

Successive moments, instance to instance, compose the poems in their whole extension. If this is so, we may object, what keeps the action as a whole from simply hanging in the air, moment upon moment from accumulating into an inchoate mass? And, again, why doesn't the lack of any date or external time reference produce the effect of a colossal abstraction?

This is obviously not the case. Why not? The reason is that these constituent moments are perceived as part and parcel of natural time. Any occurrence is so presented as to fill a portion of the passing day; hence an action that is contained within a sequence of decisive days.

We come here to a characteristic aspect of the Homeric story. Unlike any other large-scale epic, that I know of, it is conceived in terms of the days of which it consists. The number of days can be counted. Thus, in the *Iliad* the fighting days are no more than five (cp. 2.48, 7.421, 8.1, 8.485, 11.1, 19.1);

preceded by the ten days of the plague which occasion Achilles' wrath (1.53–54); twelve needed for Zeus' response to Thetis' plea on behalf of her son (1.493); and followed, on the other hand, by the day of Patroclus' funeral games (23.226); another twelve for Hector's ransom to be decided upon (24.31); and one more for the actual return of Hector's corpse (24.695). Similarly, in the *Odyssey*: five days are allowed to Telemachus to reach Sparta on his quest (cp. 2.1, 3.1, 404, 491, 4.306); one day (5.1) for the gods to decide on Odysseus' return; another five days (cp. 5.228, 263) for Odysseus to build his raft; another twenty (cp. 279, 388–90) to reach Scheria; three days spent there (cp. 6.48, 8.1, 13.18, 93); and six more in Ithaca, to win back his household (cp. 15.56, 189, 495, 17.1, 20.91 23.347).

These days, however, are not to be looked upon realistically, as if each of them were the plausible duration of what it contains. How could we conceive, for instance, the great day included in *Iliad* 11–18? The ebb and flow of battle, the rout of the Achaeans, the death of Sarpedon, the death of Patroclus, the struggle over their bodies—could this and much else happen all in one day? There is obviously no question of literal duration. A kinship of form and content compels these events to share the same day.

What matters more than the number of days is a sense of the day's presence, the visualization of events in their daylight occurrence, the fact that any part of the story is presented as something taking place before our eyes. As in a play (and in ordinary life), what we see taking place inevitably merges with our awareness of the actual day. But on a far larger scale than in a play, and quite unlike ordinary life, each event is removed from the incidental entanglements of daily living, is simplified, condensed, and seen in its momentary and yet monumental isolation.

The day thus lights up the scenes of the action and keeps them in chime. In *Iliad* 1, for instance, we see in immediate succession Odysseus returning Chryseis to her father, the Achaeans cleansing themselves of the plague, the envoys of Agamemnon seizing Briseis, Achilles entreating Thetis. There is no need to break the narrative into chapters, to introduce transitions or work up changes of atmosphere and environment. Nor is there any need for chronological plausibility. Continuity of time and contiguity of place are here sufficient. The same daylight evidence confers reality upon each of these events and brings them together in relation with one another. A mere conjunction is enough to mark any transition from one topic to the next. It is as if we were driven on by the flux of existence and not by the plot.

Thus, throughout the poems, day succeeds day, binding the action to the earth. A definite duration of time contains every happening. But such time does not merely provide an external frame. No, it is internal to the action itself: it endows it with its rapid measure; it simplifies it into moments. As though the day itself composed the story, we have less a plot than events which conspire by sharing the same air and the same space. Or we might better say that the plot is continually absorbed into daily existence and vice versa. The poet keeps a most delicate balance between the two. It is extraordinary how a sense of unity comes from sheer juxtaposition. Act reverberates upon act, scene upon scene, as surely as day follows day, as if unwittingly building up the large outline of the story.

VI

We may wonder why it was that the poems took this singular form, why this sense of time encompassed the subject matter so pervasively and intimately. The crux of the matter lay in harmonizing the time of human experience and that of nature, in allowing moments of life to go hand in hand with day and night. The human moment could not be abstracted. It had to be seen in its natural context.

We thus return to what is most essential in the poems—the fact that the principal motive and starting point in both was an overriding human moment: the wrath of Achilles in the *Iliad*, Odysseus' yearning to return home in the *Odyssey*. For the plight of these two heroes could not be taken for granted. It had to be realized, shown dramatically—that is to say, visualized in its concrete incidents, fully exposed at certain specific points of space and time. But what kind of time reference was involved here? It is the time of nature, the present day. We are always made aware of the day's course when we see Odysseus in tears gazing out to the sea from Calypso's shore, building his raft, sailing; and, equally so, when we see Achilles raging in the assembly, withdrawing to his tent, crushed by Patroclus' death. Here were dramatic scenes freshly enacted rather than descriptive details of a hero's career; here were turning points of the story, focal moments conditioning the course of events and made all the more striking by their condensation within the span of a few days. All the rest of the narrative could not help but be drawn into their orbit, transformed into moments of activity riding on the same wave of time.

The days, as few as they are long, flow over the whole large canvas of the poems; war and peace are resolved into spontaneous scenes following one another and subject to the same rhythm of existence as the central dramas of Achilles and Odysseus, as in a play. In Shakespeare's *Henry IV*, for instance, we find the tavern scenes side by side with the major events. But Homer could not rely in the same way on the imaginative plausibility of character, on history and politics working in unison. He could not, by virtue of these realities, disregard the natural time of the action. What he did was to transform a timeless myth into human acts running their course; and, in so doing, he could only find in nature itself—a sequence of days and nights—the pervasive, unifying thread.

VII

The very theme was dramatic. Both poems begin with an irruption into the vast epic material. The war of Troy, its origin and aftermath, could not but give way to what now filled the poet's imagination: the rising passion of a man at its breaking point. Here a radical and vital element asserted its deep human logic, expunging or bringing into unison with itself the surrounding mythologies, as the gods and fate and the whole heroic world all appeared to be involved in the present issue. We have, on the one hand, a crucial, absorbing moment in a man's life and, on the other, the universe held in corresponding suspense. The timeless, immortal gods are quickened by a keener sense. The outlying world of nature comes into the picture as the immediate scene for a central human event.

This sense of time may thus be appreciated from the viewpoint of its human significance. Achilles and Odysseus are not heroes celebrated for glory's sake; they do not work their way through the paths of myth and history. They are completely involved in instant experience. What matters is their momentary presence and the intensity of its impact, which is due to concentration in time. Here is the mainspring of a quickening movement in the whole action of the poems. A like stress, a like urgency necessarily affects all the characters, seen as they are in one brief moment of climax. The human burden of looking at things this way is well expressed by Sarpedon when he tells Glaucus (*Il.* 12.322ff.):

> Dear friend, if even now / we could escape from this
>   war
> and ever were we to live / free from old age and from
>   death,
> then indeed neither would I / be fighting here right in
>   front
> nor would I send you forth / to the battle-where-men-
>   win-glory.
> But now since anyway / the spirits of death are upon
>   us
> in thousands, and none of us / can either escape or
>   avoid them,
> go we, whether another / our lives may claim or we his.

Hence the sharp feeling of mortality throughout the poems, the sympathy of humanized gods, the abridgment of the mythical.

But it is the form itself which, more than any statement, bears the message. The flash of existence comes again and again in countless instances side by side with the main action. Be it emotion or sheer movement or position, it always typifies a moment of life rather than instructing or developing the plot or simply stirring our curiosity. Any occasion, whatever its narrative purpose may be, acquires a human and tragic significance through the very fact of being so fully present and yet so inevitably transient.

Here we find most clear before us Homer's singularity. Other epic poets, or novelists, do indeed give us moments of a character's life against a larger background; but in Homer there is no background or foreground. Once the action is given its decisive spark in the images of Achilles and Odysseus, the same impulse is pursued apace and everyone else is similarly driven into the limelight: Agamemnon, Nestor,

Paris, Menelaus, Helen, Diomedeș—all have their moment of glory. Even those only mentioned once are presented in the same way. The relative importance of each lies in the degree of impact made rather than in what the poet may explicitly say.

VIII

We may also look at the sense of time in more general terms, to see how it contributed to the great scale of the poems. It should not be looked upon in mere quantitative terms, in that moment added to moment necessarily produced a composition of large dimensions. Let us consider, rather, the sense of development, the growth itself. What comes to the fore is the *nature* of the moment: how resilient each momentary act is, how naturally it impels the next one into the limelight, and how inevitably the whole sequence leads us to a final climax and denouement.

We have, therefore, no leisurely account such as that of a tale which begins "Once upon a time." Nor does the abstract interest of the topic lead us on from cause to effect, regardless of any specific time sequence. There is a definite starting point, an initial movement that precipitates all subsequent events. It is as though the action, once set in motion, could not be stopped. The poet himself points to such a compelling moment right at the beginning of each poem (cp. *Il.* 1.5, *Od.* 1.10). "When the year came in the revolving of seasons," he says more specifically about the time of Odysseus' return (*Od.* 1.16). But why the need to mention the years, the seasons? Why not say simply "once" or mention some fictitious, mythological date? Because there must be a certain day (no matter the date), when a new direction is imparted to the recurring succession of cyclical time; from now on each day counts by virtue of its human interest and yet remains a natural day, bound to the regular phases of sunrise and nightfall, inevitably bringing into view the surrounding world—hence, simultaneously, the sense of general existence and the heartbeat of the human action.

Time struck the tune, as if the verse-rhythm passed into the rhythm of what actually happened. The effect is cumulative: then . . . then . . . then. . . . What is lost in variety of incident or complexity of plot is gained in persistence of form. The battle scenes follow one another at length, as do the banquets of the *Odyssey,* repeating similar patterns. Over and above the simple plot, we are made to feel the flux of existence; and yet the flux itself could not have been shown otherwise than by finding room for it within the time-span of the plot.

Hence comes breadth as well as length, an impression of strength and power quite apart from the size. How else could justice be done to the epic Muse, how else blend so simple a plot with a sense of the world's destinies? Any discursive digression would have detracted from Homer's concreteness. Only the cumulative beat of succeeding moments could produce this universal, encompassing effect within a matter of days. The repeated phrases, the repeated scenes find here their ultimate reason. They are but extreme particulars of a general trend. By highlighting form, they remove us from any narrow topic and attune us to a way of being, happening, passing away. Incident is thus absorbed into rhythm. It is as if any single moment were the epitome of all moments, as if any passing occasion were the spark of an infinite repercussion. And what is true of single instances is also true of the whole composition. The story, as if unawares, takes on a universal significance: there are other Troys, other Odyssean wanderings. And yet this truth comes from sheer poetic perception and not from any abstract idea. We have, as it were, an eternal moment: simultaneously an intense action and a paradigm of things.

IX

The process of composition, Homer's art, and the story itself are otherwise explained today on the basis of the theories of "oral poetry." What we have, according to these theories, is composition by theme. A theme, in this sense, is the narrative pattern underlying any of the basic occurrences that are common in epic poetry: it persists no matter what incidental developments there may be within the occurrence itself. The "oral poet" always bears the theme in mind. He instinctively knows it. In his need to perform rapidly before an audience, it is an indispensable means for ordering the material and composing the story.

Thus we have in Homer such frequent occurrences as the gathering of an assembly, a banquet, dressing up, departing, arriving, arming, engaging in a duel. The "oral poet" (as Homer is supposed to be) finds here a basic mold that he may refine and develop. Just as he uses formulas to build up a theme, so he uses themes to compose a larger stretch of narrative.

Such a notion of "theme" could be brought into line with a principle of form. But it is treated otherwise. The emphasis is placed upon narrative usefulness, the practical purpose of the performer. What comes to the fore is facility of versification and ready delivery. Ability, skill, and talent are all displayed in compositional technique.

We may still wonder what kind of poetic excellence informs this composition by theme. Why did these themes, no less than formulas, prove so effective? To this we get no clear answer. At best, we are told that this form of composition is sanctioned by the fact of its being traditional. The ultimate criterion lies in the abstract entity called tradition, a repository of whatever a society deems hallowed by age-old practice. Such an approach is anthropological rather than aesthetic. Insofar as poetic values are concerned, it begs the question.

We may, then, appeal to an aesthetic principle rather than to thematics. We should point not so much to a theme as to thought dwelling again and again upon its object, not so much to formulas as to love of form. We might thus come to regard this "composition by theme" not as a cultural phenomenon but as a way of looking at life.

What we must appeal to is Homer's kind of concreteness. It naturally leads us to see the action in the shape of actual incidents that have their way of occurring and recurring because this is what happens in real life. Why an assembly theme? Because it is in an assembly that confrontation most effectively takes place and feelings run high. Why an arming scene? Because a warrior is not taken for granted. His gear makes him what he is as he arms himself. Why a fighting scene in its Homeric form? Because the chaos of battle essentially comes down to an encounter, a clash, a fall. Why the themes of arrival and departure? Because these are vital junctures marking a beginning and an end. Why the theme of return? Because it condenses what in life are instances of recovery, restoration, revival, coming into one's own. Or why a hero's wrath? Because it is the kind of crisis that provides any story with its necessary tension.

Homer carries to an extreme point this process of complex simplification. He fixes each occurrence in its pertinent setting. It would not do to have the quarrel between Achilles and Agamemnon take place in some hidden corner of the camp or locate a feat of arms in some mountain gorge of the vicinity. The same applies to emotions or states of mind. Odysseus, like Achilles, grieves on the solitary shore looking

out to sea: we would hardly find him indulging his melancholy just anywhere. For whereas random episodes could
befit an arbitrary description, here any happening is inextricably bound to its ground and occasion by the nature of what
it fundamentally must be. Hence the vitality of form: form
drawing from life a quickening outline, life finding its consistency in form.

This sense of form and life appeals to the modern reader
as it did to the ancients. It accounts for a plot so simple and
a composition so large, for the momentary occasions and their
wide significance, for the many recurrences and the narrative
intent, for what is both an epic and a mirror of life's consis-
tencies.

III CHARACTERS

I

If immediate acts make up the story step by step, it follows that they also make up the characters so brought into play. Homer does not see his characters in the light of any alleged biography or long-range career. They hardly seem to exist outside the actual occasion of what they say or do.

Nowhere is this integration of character and action more complete than in Homer. The first lines of the poem give us an idea: Achilles one with his wrath; Odysseus, one with his tantalizing return. In the proem of other epics this is not so: in the *Aeneid,* for instance, the image of Aeneas is elusive, absorbed into shadowy perspectives of history.

Homer plunges us into the very essence of character. He brings us back to the source. For how do we realize character in our own lives? By observing people in action. We hardly ever take personal characteristics for granted, categorizing under their heading anyone we may know—at least, not in moments of clear perception. In such moments, it is action that reveals character and not vice versa; or at least, it might be said, we hardly distinguish between the two. To anyone who is not a slave to stereotypes, the notion of character comes from a sense of being, acting, living. We perceive a pose, a movement, a voice, a shape; and, if the impression is strong enough, a full-fledged person stands exposed to the mind's eye. The image itself will be fraught with meaning. Character in its broadest and deepest sense shows through it.

Homer thus realizes character in a fundamental way. We should forget for a while all generalizations about the "hero" or "Homeric man" and look, rather, at the individual action in itself and by itself—how it comes about as a tension of mind and limb responding to an immediate need, how it brings into play the whole of a person's resourcefulness and strength, how elemental is its nature, how radical the alternatives it offers—to strike or be struck, resist or escape, accept or refuse—and always on occasions that are not casual but set life at stake. It is at such points that a hero takes up a position for all he is worth—that is to say, reveals himself as a character.

Recurring instances do not, by their uniformity, nullify the differentiations of character. On the contrary, they show how variations arise from one basic mold, how individual experiences are grafted onto solid fact, how even the most fitful movement is made vital by being rooted in common ground. Thus any basic act, insofar as it is externalized, necessarily appears the same on all occasions but differs in its motivation or its impact according to time and place, and according to who is acting or is acted upon. The minstrel regularly sings at Ithaca or Scheria; yet the same singing produces different reactions, creating different characters on the spur of the moment. In the battle scenes, the same clash and fall reverberates in different ways, eliciting potential or actual characters from among the stalwart warriors.

There is sameness in the occasions, but distinction in their resonance. And this is where the perspicuity of the Homeric action comes into play: just as the characters hardly exist outside the action, so nothing happens that is not perceived or actually realized. This is to say that nothing is a mere descriptive theme, that anything that happens is dramatized and decisively affects those who are present. The exposure of a place, the ripeness of a moment, are of paramount importance. They turn recurrence into experience. We see character produced by the raw materials of existence, by the very interaction of things.

II

A case in point is Ajax. We find him in *Il.* 7.211ff., responding to Hector's challenge:

> Such Ajax arose the-huge-one, / a bulwark-he-to-the-Achaeans,
> a smile on his grim dark face, / whilst on his feet below
> he formed long steps in his stride, / waving the long-shadowed spear.
>
> . . . .
> Closer did Ajax advance / bearing his shield like a tower
> the brazen seven-fold shield. . . .

A firm, massive figure, fleeting self-consciousness surfacing in the grim smile: it is as if we witnessed the mass touched into life. Here is self-contained strength ready to be tested; no movement is taken for granted. And the great, towering shield contributes to the effect, giving the final touch to Ajax as "bulwark of the Achaeans."

Again and again we have the impression of unyielding raw material. In *Il.* 16.104–05, his helmet emits a dreadful din on being struck, as though walls were being pounded by a battering-ram. In 8.267ff., the archer Teucer shoots as he peeps from under the edge of the great shield and then sinks back behind Ajax's body as if it were a place of refuge. In

17.746ff., the hero is compared to a promontory that checks a river's mounting flood and channels it down to the plain.

What predominates is the moment of resistance. Rather than an outburst, a resolution scarcely aware of itself—rather than reckless attack, a solid stance. Or, if retreat is inevitable, it is gradual, as if instinctively measured against the possibilities of resistance, as in *Il.* 11.546ff.:

> Dumbstruck he stood; on his back / he threw the seven-hide shield,
> and fled glancing round / at the throng, as a wild beast would do,
> back turning step after step,—knee slightly shifting with knee.

And a little later (*Il.* 558ff.):

> As at a field's edge a donkey, / walks on, braving children that check him,
> a sluggard upon whose back / many a staff was broken in two;
> into the rich crop he enters, / wasting, and there the children
> strike upon him with staffs, / but utterly vain is their strength;
> hardly at last do they drive him, / when filled he is with the fodder;
> so upon Ajax-the-great, / upon Ajax-the-son-of-Telamon
> closed the great-hearted Trojans / and their far-famed allies,
> knocking with spikes mid-shield, / knocking and ever pursuing.

To resist or give way—life finds its path between such basic alternatives. It is a matter of delicate balance. Ajax's characterization grows accordingly: from the friction of opposing motions the human shape acquires its own identity. It is as though the surrounding stress forged the hero's mold, as though the experiences of blow and counterblow were immediately transformed into endurance, resilience, and willpower.

Untested potential lies concealed in the hero's bulk, ready to be sparked off by divine influence, as when, at Poseidon's touch, he says (*Il.* 13.77ff.):

> round the spear resistless my hands
> quiver, within me / a might is astir, and my feet
> are driven.

Later (15.686ff.), as Ajax defends the ships, leaping from deck to deck, what again stands out is the leap itself, as striking as that of a circus-rider who springs from one horse to another. The sudden nimbleness of the great body cannot be taken for granted, the exceptional feat needs to be set in bold relief.

Such a character does not speak much. If he does so, it is to give voice to the spirit of resistance already implicit in his frame, as in *Il.* 15.733ff.:

> Be men, my friends. . . .
> Do you think any helpers there are / any helpers left
>   here behind you
> or a wall or a bastion / to ward off doom from the men?
> No, no city is close by, / no city buttressed with walls.
> In our hands is all hope. [Cp. 15.502ff.; 12.269ff.;
>   15.501, 561; 17.716ff.]

The very imagery Ajax evokes seems to symbolize what he actually is, a human barrier like a wall, a fortress, a rampart.

Shape or image produces character; and the character becomes more transparent from appearance to appearance. Hence there is a natural consistency in the development that is carried far, even beyond the battle scenes. It is no wonder that in the *Embassy* Ajax is forestalled by Odysseus in speaking to Achilles first (*Il.* 9.223), and, at the end, he only marks patience, endurance, resignation in the failure (9.624–42). It is a fine last touch that, in *Od.* 11.543, Ajax's ghost stands silently aloof. Odysseus, who balked him of Achilles' arms and drove him to suicide, gets no word from him. "He would have spoken," Odysseus tells the Phaeacians, "had I not turned elsewhere." For the last time, there is a potential untapped capacity in this compact figure.

III

Hector stands as a counterpart to Ajax. What we immediately see of him is his nimbleness and lightness, as in *Il.* 11.62ff.:

> Just as out of the clouds / appears an ominous star
> bright-shining, and then again / it sinks into shadows
>   of clouds,
> so would instantly Hector / now amid the foremost
>   appear
> and then again in the rear . . .

Thus, more than once, the same forthright and decisive movement (*Il.* 5.494, 6.103, 11.211ff.):

> And, at once, from the chariot, / in arms he sprang to
>   the ground;
> swaying the sharp two spears / he went each way
>   through the host
> urging them on to the battle, / and so stirred up the
>   dread war-cry;

they all rallied about, / and stood in front of the
Achaeans.

No wonder, then, that we see Hector in the greatest variety
of positions, as when he leaves the battlefield for the city (*Il.*
6.116ff.):

All at once having spoken / Hector-helmet-shining
departed;
upon his neck it kept knocking, / and upon his legs,
the dark hide—
the rim whose outermost edge / ran round the shield-
richly-embossed

or as when he assays the foe (*Il.* 13.806):

upon the edge of their ranks / he tested them stepping
forth.

Quite alien to him is any *aristeia* or succession of heroic exploits. Rather, he is here and there, near and far, often summoned from one place to another in the hour of need—a
shimmering, fitful, pervasive presence. So Shakespeare pic-
tured him (*Troilus and Cressida*, 5.5.19–29):

There is a thousand Hectors in the field;
now here he fights on Galathe his horse,
and there lacks work; anon he's there afoot

. . . .

Here, there, and everywhere he leaves and takes;
dexterity so obeying appetite
that what he will he does, and does so much
that proof is called impossibility.

The treatment, though with opposite effect, is like that of
Ajax. Here are basic movements responding to an immediate

need; here is a function taking its form. Why is Hector so mobile? Because as defender of a besieged city he must make himself available everywhere. And why is he so forceful, so personal even at this basic level? It is, again, a question of focus. The persistent touch creates intensity within the type. How symptomatic are those sudden displacements, that leap from the chariot, that figure vanishing in the distance! His resilience always matches the occasion; it is neither in excess nor default; by being so true and consistent, it ensures the vitality of the picture. It is as if Hector were conjured up by each occurrence as it occurs. He is nowhere described, but gesture or movement produces the figure and gives it contour.

This mobility of body is also a mobility of spirit. Paris thus characterizes Hector in answering his rebuke (*Il.* 3.60ff.): "Ever within you the heart is as unworn as an axe that cleaves right through the timber at the hands of a man . . . enhancing the swing of his body." Homer's sense of animate energy precludes any nice distinction between body and mind, facilitating the swift characterization. Hector is nimble, ready, sharp, keen, open, self-exposed, and, by the same token, unguarded and vulnerable. Yet Homer would hardly use such predicates, implied as they are in pure relevance of form and movement.

The mere representation of a figure in motion thus gives us a cue. Hector's character is achieved by the simplest means: the sheer recurrence of certain positions and motions that become typical of what he is and set him in high relief. We have his swift advances in books 8–16 and his no less swift retreats (cp. *Il.* 11.61ff., 12.437f.; 16.656ff.; 20.379ff.); twice we find him at the threshold of life and death (11.354ff.; 14.418ff.); and, in 15.239ff., it is as if he were resurrected from limbo. Hence he is weak and strong, by turns, shattered and triumphant, courageous and panic-stricken—but always human, all-too-human. Again and again a movement forward and backward, an advance and a withdrawal, a tantalizing victory and a defeat. It is so up to the last: the stand before Achilles, the sudden flight, the ultimate resistance and death. Action, character, fate are all one—recurring predicament that becomes more and more tense down to the bitter end.

And what is more, the same kind of treatment applies to Hector within the walls of Troy—especially so in the dialogue with Andromache (*Il.* 6.406ff.). She would not let him go and be killed. "Hector," she says, "you are to me father and bountiful mother, you are my brother, yes, and flowering husband." What again emerges is a moment of concentrated truth. To bereft Andromache, Hector is indeed quite literally all these things; but to us the apostrophe suddenly reveals him as a many-faceted and yet self-contained person.

And now Hector's versatility grows inwardly. It deepens to the intimate realm of life. "Your thoughts are mine," he replies to her, "but I am ashamed before the Trojans and the long-robed women of Troy, if like a weakling I dodge." How natural and unassuming is this sense of shame. But then he has a second thought: how he learned to be brave, the paternal heritage. Here lies his life, his destiny asserting itself against hope, "for I know in my heart and my mind that sacred Ilium . . . will fall." City, people, family—in the next moment even these loyalties recede. Something deeper and more personal takes over. For nothing matters in comparison with what he now sees in his mind's eye: Andromache led away in captivity. It is as though the truth of the emotion were prophetic. But doom is no sooner envisaged than it is spirited away. The radiant child is there, suddenly drawing all the focus, bringing hope. "May he be even as I am and stand high among the Trojans," Hector prays, his earlier premonition of evil quite inundated by a new wave of life. "Oh, do not grieve overmuch," he finally says to his wife, "fate cannot be but what it is, no one escapes it who is born, be he strong or weak; in its spite I shall never be killed." Troy, Andromache, and their son are thus cast in a larger perspective. A little later, with Paris, Hector indulges, for a moment, in the wishful prospect of Troy's deliverance.

This is no memorable speech all of a piece, no character completely absorbed in his duty. We have, rather, a succession of impressions. The scene, in spite of impending doom, has an airy quality about it produced by thoughts that freely flow in response to the moment. What contradictions there are stem from a deeper logic than the obvious one; they are none other than life's shimmering light and shade. Hence the initially tragic tone resolved into sudden joy and then into contemplative vistas. There are tears and there is laughter. Hector is supple, articulate, free, sensitive, delicate, and strong. It is as if the nimbleness of the battlefield were here transformed into finer susceptibilities. Yet we recognize in him the same openness, the same predisposition to meet the fleeting occasion.

Compare Hector's soliloquy before he fights Achilles (*Il.* 22.99ff.). Courage is not taken for granted. It makes its way with pain. Fluctuations and alternatives stand out: to escape, to repair to the city? Ah, shame; to talk peace with Achilles? Ah, vanity: there is no dallying with such a man, as a boy and girl might dally in some country place. Nothing is left but to win or die. Here again no memorable heroic speech on virtue or glory. Again a similar plasticity of thought—or thoughts turning to imaginings—no precepts, maxims, statements, or ready-made resolutions.

Hector is the most human of the heroes in the *Iliad*. One obvious reason is that we see him at home, in close relation with his family and people. This, however, is not my point. It would be utterly inadequate to say that Hector is a typical husband, father, son, and soldier, for none of these roles is taken for granted. They are caught at their delicate points of realization; and these points converge, summoning up a comprehensive image. Each instance tells us what it is to be a man in any of these concurring and blending capacities.

As a result, Hector appears quite removed from the mythical background. In book 6 of the *Iliad*, for instance, he is as natural as anyone could be. We might, then, expect him to behave like any modern character endowed with definite likes and dislikes, idiosyncrasies, and other realistic traits. But this is obviously not so. Why not? Because the heroic may be humanized, but not converted into anything willful or whimsical. Homer only deals with basic conditions of life; and equally basic are his characters, inseparable as they are from the instances which bring them into being. Hector thus solely exists and lives through the action intrinsic to him. It would not do to see him behaving at random, being fastidious or morose or titillated by anything in particular. No, the full moment of experience absorbs him entirely, even if it is resolved in the lightness of a smile or a passing gesture: action or state of being rather than behavior. Within the brief succession of days that see Hector alive, there is no room for asides or extemporizing to bring out any supernumerary trait.

The integration of character and action is here carried to an extreme. Hector is made self-evident step after step. No particular attitude of his should be attributed to predetermined characteristics or to external motives. Why, for instance, his love for Helen (cp. *Il.* 24.762, 6.360)? Fondness, inclination? A chivalrous temperament? The reason lies, rather, in the fact itself. Helen's beauty is no arbitrary matter. She is a shining presence; the spell she casts, as well as its

attending woe, are established in the ways of nature and fate.
And it is not for Hector to sit in judgment. He has heard her
cry (*Il.* 6.344ff.), as he has Andromache's. Being so imaginatively responsive, how could he not sympathize with her
plight? One might say, at any rate, that the baffling truth of
human relations strikes corresponding chords in himself.

The mystery of character is thus entwined with that of
events. Again, why, we may ask, does Hector rebuke Paris so
sharply only to be reconciled with him a little later (cp. *Il.*
3.76, 6.521ff., 13.788)? Or why is he so stung and yet sobered
by the reproaches of Sarpedon and Glaucus (cp. *Il.* 5.493,
17.170ff.)? Or why is he so impatient with Polydamas only to
regret it at the last moment (*Il.* 22.100)? Levity or recklessness?
No, here is versatility, which on each occasion comes to terms
with the truth of things; here is malleability and freedom of
spirit. For we know how strains of character spontaneously
arise from the brunt of experience, how events test and shape
a man's temper when he fully meets their challenge and tastes
life to the core.

One might object that what I have said about Hector as
a warrior could also apply to other Homeric heroes: such as
the advance and retreat between Troy and the ships, or
the desperate alternatives of life and death (cp. Odysseus in
Il. 11.401ff., Menelaus in 17.90ff., and especially Agenor in
21.552ff.).

But it is not a question of who does what. It is, rather, a
question of form. What is true of others is true of Hector in a
particular way. His appearances gather momentum, giving
him a different kind of richness and intensity. Characterization here starts from a common core. It means establishing

an identity, individualizing, defining and deepening a universal trend.

What loomed in the poet's mind, we may suppose, was
the image of a man both defiant and vulnerable, both attacking impetuously and falling into the ambush of defeat or
death. Here was a basic image intrinsic to the subject matter.
But sink such an image into the actualities of the struggle,
make it conversant with the fortunes of a beleaguered city, let
it be fully involved in all occasions, both propitious and ad-
verse, and it will become increasingly articulate, familiar, and
personal.

As far as aesthetic appreciation is concerned, it makes no
difference whether we have to do with tradition or with individual invention. We must ultimately posit the same perceptual process somewhere, sometime. For we have, in any
case, a broadening idea rather than aggregated matter and
motley multiplicity. Thus, in the work of a major artist the
same figure often surfaces again and again, rehearsing in
more or less perfected form some basic idea—as, say, in Mi-
chelangelo's *Slaves*. Indeed, no vital form is so finite and self-
sufficient as not to prefigure or intimate likenesses of itself.

So it is in Homer. There are potential Hectors everywhere
on the battlefield; but it is Sarpedon who most suggests Hector's image: see his fight with Tlepolemus in *Iliad* 5, his faint-
ing and reviving (5.696ff.), his death at the hands of Patroclus
(16.482ff.)—all of which parallels crucial events of Hector's
rise and fall. Or look at Asius in *Iliad* 12: his charge through
the Achaean rampart is like a rehearsal of what Hector will
do. Or, again, consider Glaucus: is he not, in turn, a shadow
of Sarpedon, a sweetened version of the same type?

Here, then, is a powerful ingredient in Hector's human
and nonmythical makeup: the fact that he grows out of vital

raw material. What source could be more radical, direct, or effective in the shaping of character? We find, at bottom, a sense of natural energies which are as general as they are capable of being more particularly defined in single instances. Most distinctively suggestive must have been that resilience of limb and spirit which Homer perceived so keenly in animal motions. The process of falling and rising, of abatement and recovery, attains in Hector the fullest outline, developing and being refined into character. Hence, all at once, his vulnerability and strength and self-renewing elasticity. The sheer resourcefulness of existence appears intensified by being so concentrated in one person.

IV

In other cases, the process of characterization was more strenuous, the mythical background more pervasive and harder to humanize. We still find the same concrete treatment of the action, but the achievement was no less than to blend into one clear personality the frailty of a man and the spell of a god. Such is the case with Achilles. As the son of the sea-goddess Thetis, he is a constant object of divine concern and yet, born mortal, he is plunged by his love for Patroclus into a human struggle that leads him to die young.

It is in the spirit of Homer's concreteness and sense of truth that he did not make Achilles an invincible hero. His man-to-man combats are essentially no different from those of other warriors. There is nothing here of other myths that tell us about his invulnerability or the attempts to make him immortal; nothing of superhuman exploits performed, even in his childhood. In Homer, Achilles is, as he says himself, the most miserable of men. How, then, did Homer resolve this contrast? How did he bring out an extraordinary divine quality within this all-too-human frame?

The first lines of the *Illiad* give us a clue: "Sing to me, o goddess, the wrath of Achilles that brought countless woes. . . ." We are immediately removed from mere exploits and introduced, rather, to the dynamics of action and reaction. The purview is qualitative, not quantitative. A momentous interplay of forces is suddenly unloosed. Relations, implications, complications naturally arise; and Achilles is placed right at the center as catalyst and affected object, moved and mover, agent and victim. The importance of Achilles is thus internal to the event. It is to be measured according to the resulting drama and not on the strength of heroic deeds that can be enumerated or compared. It is a matter of inner tensions being immediately translated into actions. Hence, also, the insistence on the emotional moment—not so much the man, but his wrath, and later his grief. For it is in the nature of such passions to set things astir and reverberate incessantly.

Being so steeped in overwhelming experiences, how could Achilles not show all the frailties of a man? And being at the same time so pivotal a figure whose very hesitations are like fate held in balance, how could he not cast a godlike spell? He is in the position of a man who is in jeopardy and yet is suddenly charged with colossal responsibilities.

Such is Achilles' unique position. And yet it is never abstracted in terms of cause and effect; it is native to his image. The representation of Achilles is no less concrete than that of Ajax and Hector: he is not described either; we see him in a series of mighty, self-contained scenes. But, every time, his position is such as to have the most sweeping effects, which naturally rebound upon himself and thus contribute to his power as a character. The explosion of his wrath brings about Agamemnon's delusion; his rejection of Agamemnon's overtures is immediately followed by Hector's onslaught and the

Achaean rout; his yielding to Patroclus' entreaties results in sending his friend out to fight and die at the hands of Hector, whence the revenge and the reversal in the fortunes of war. And each happening, though fundamentally affecting the plot, brings out a corresponding disposition in the man until we are finally given his full dimensions. The hero must have loomed in the poet's mind along with each of these occasions—as if the concurrence of events had no other reason than to bring Achilles into focus and as if, on the other hand, Achilles himself appears as what he is on the strength of the events that gave him high relief.

Concrete instances, again, build up the character, but in this case they gather together in themselves the threads of the poem—as in a play, except that here we have the enveloping sense of the surrounding world; or as in a story presenting us with the principal incidents of a character's life, except that the dramatization is here compressed within a few days and precludes all long-drawn-out narrative or description.

In Homer, then, character arises from the fluid action, not from any single issue as it does in drama. At the same time, character is not described or developed at length. How did Homer supply that unity which, say, in a drama like the *Ajax* of Sophocles is favored by the simplicity of the issue? And how does he, on the other hand, provide that sense of many-faceted experience, change, and development which, in a story or novel, comes from envisaging a longer lapse of time?

Again the answer lies in the Homeric sense of concreteness. The unity comes from the strong presentation of the hero's image, which remains essentially the same in the way it is summoned up throughout the poem. The sense of transforming time, on the other hand, comes from the radically different situations into which the hero is drawn through the action. True as this is of all the Homeric characters, it is most clearly evident in Achilles.

Consider first the solid persistence of his image. There is, of course, the ever-recurring figure with the spell of its epithets; and there are echoes, resonances, nonliteral recurrences, like keynotes to a momentum that amplifies as the action goes on. The man who right at the beginning of the poem (*Il.* 1.151ff.) cries out to Agamemnon:

> Not I for the sake of the Trojans / for their spearmen's sake did I come
>
> hither against them to fight; / in nothing they are guilty to me;
>
> for never they drove out my oxen, / and no, nor ever my horses,
>
> nor ever did they in Phthia / the-rich-clodded-mother-of-men
>
> plunder the fruit of the land, / since in between very many
>
> shadowy mountains there are / and the resounding sea;
> but you, o shameless man, / did we follow. . . .

is naturally the same who later, rejecting Agamemnon's offers, laments the futility of the struggle, saying (9.325ff.):

> . . . many sleepless nights did I camp,
>
> many days of bloodshed I lived / through all their length waging war
>
> against men that were fighting / in the defense of their wives.
>
> . . . .
> . . . Why should they fight against Troy,

the Achaeans? And why led he / the people all here
  assembled,
the son of Atreus? Ah, was it / for the sake of Helen-
  fair-tressed?
Is it they only that cherish / their wives among human-
  kind
the sons of Atreus? No, all / that have any strength,
  any feeling
cherish their own. . . .

And the same accent can be heard when, at the end, Achilles
says to Priam (24.540ff.):

                                        . . . nor do I
attend on my father growing old, / since far away from
  my land
I sit out here in Troy / bringing woe to your children
  and you.

And consider, further, Achilles' radically different states
of being throughout the poem: his tremendous wrath when
face to face with Agamemnon; his inexorable aloofness face
to face with the Achaean envoys; his crushing grief at the
death of Patroclus; his wild revenge on Hector; his calm jo-
viality at the funeral games; his unexpected compassion before Priam. These states of mind transpire within only a
month's time, and yet they seem worlds apart from one another. We are so immersed in the moments of realization that
we hardly notice the lack of passing time which narrative
plausibility would seem to require.

For such a treatment to be effective, the image had to be
solid yet malleable. While steadfastly abiding in his heroic
mold, Achilles also had to appear as a man wholly committed

to his role and transfigured by it in each instance—as if each instance were a final and decisive ordeal. In this way, what we might otherwise only be able to conceive as a gradual development could be evinced on the strength of a few crucial occasions. Intensity had to substitute for extensiveness. The sheer depth of the involvement gives us the sense of a life-encompassing experience.

We should thus give each appearance of Achilles its full-est significance. The first scene of his wrath is not a mere question of "heroic honor"; we must give full weight, rather, to the human, or animal, element underlying the heroic. There is booty to be taken, a woman to be possessed, a war to be fought; what could be more primitive, low, and down-to-earth? Honor, if there is any, is indistinguishable from pos-sessive instinct, stolid self-assertiveness, and sexual lust. En-croachment upon any of these touches to the quick a mainspring of life. When Agamemnon takes Briseis, it is as if Achilles suffered a gash in his very being. This favorite of the gods is turned into an outcast. But the human develop-ment is equally momentous. Because Achilles withdraws and seems reduced to impotence, his self-assertion must take a different path: it becomes a vindication of his own self. Why should he fight this war? He is driven to question all issues by the dramatic moment that bursts around him. It is as though he were born again from the ashes of discomfiture, as though we witnessed the way in which spirit takes shape out of the very slime of existence. For here are seething in-stincts which impart the first spark of life to a character be-fore it is conscious of itself—instincts which, being thwarted, broaden and yield to a sovereign sense of irony. The blind, self-assertive will reaches for higher levels of consciousness.

Achilles' monumental aloofness in book 9 is no less rad-ical. In rejecting Agamemnon's overtures, this supreme warrior disavows all warlike ambition. He will sail for home the following day. A wife of his native country, peace, the bounteousness of life— he yearns for nothing else. He momentarily grasps in his imagination that fullness of life which the fates have denied him.

Then comes the crushing grief over Patroclus' death— grief that blots out his earlier wrath as well as all thoughts of home. He is again a changed man. "Oh, might I be dead even now," he cries, "since I was not there with my friend when he was killed." Notice how the mythical theme of a short but glorious life is here transformed into a strain of character. For now Achilles *wants* to die. What is mortality for him? Not merely an inevitable condition, but a way of being and an essential quality of life. The thought of death is now one with his love. Nothing else matters any more. He vindicates in his own way this newly discovered human value when he cries out to his divine mother (*Il.* 18.86ff.):

> Oh would that there out at sea / in the midst of the nymphs never dying
> you had stayed, would that Peleus / had married a mortal wife.
> But now it is even your lot / to be fraught with an infinite pain
> for the death of your son. . . .

In saying this, Achilles rejects all divine sublimity. We have a moment of utter humanization. If he lives yet a little longer, it is only to avenge Patroclus by killing Hector. And now the ancient savagery seizes him again, as he maims Hector's corpse and sacrifices Trojan youths on Patroclus' pyre. "He offends the mute earth in his rage," says Apollo to the horrified gods.

All the more amazing is Achilles' last scene with Priam,

who has come to ransom his son's corpse. He is shocked, moved, sobered by the old man's presence, and he weeps, reflects, thinks aloud. It is, one might say, Achilles' last epiphany; we could hardly expect him to fight again after this.

Are we any closer to Achilles as a character? The twofold aspect of heroic solidity and radical transformation is symptomatic. What it means in respect to character is simultaneous power and vulnerability, the same high degree of pertinacity and susceptibility. The ebb and flow of circumstance generate in him a corresponding tension. The drift of events thus both gives him life and destroys him. He is consumed by his own fire.

Power, with Achilles, hangs in the balance. It is no matter of external authority. It is a *sense* of power, or a feeling of destiny in what he says or does. It is, in other words, internalized, intrinsic to the experienced moment. For what happens is clearly beyond his control; and yet he has, in the darkness, an unerring instinct to strike most effectively at a decisive point, whatever the consequences may be. Beyond his awareness or command, the truth of emotions has its sway, precipitating the flow of events.

Such is the case when, right at the beginning, Achilles makes the decision to call the assembly (*Il.* 1.55):

> for in his mind she put it / Hera-the-goddess-white-armed.

Here is a thought which is free, simple, unequivocal, god-inspired. It goes right to the mark. We are made to feel that a supreme issue is at stake, commensurate to the hero and the god, pertaining both to the clarity of human action and to the mysteries of fate. Hence the forthright tone in the proposal that the seer be consulted, the determination to stand by him even if his response should offend Agamemnon—to stand by him, as he says, "as long as I live, as long as my eyes have sight on the earth." Is this courage, piety, or policy? None of these, but, rather, the capacity of a vital response, a readiness that cannot brook delays and sets Achilles forthwith upon a fatal course. We would hardly expect such a step from the prudent Odysseus or from the simple and warlike Ajax.

Or we may look at Achilles after the scene of wrath, as he dashes the sceptre to the ground and cries out (*Il.* 1.234ff.):

> Yes indeed by this sceptre; / never from it will branches or leaves
> put forth since when it first / left on the mountains its stump
> nor will it bloom again ever . . .
> a longing, yes, for Achilles / shall seize the sons of the Achaeans.

Both the words and the gesture seem to match the irrevocable ways of nature, portending the future.

Or take his rejection of Agamemnon's envoys in *Iliad* 9. They approach him as if he were an angry god, even going so far as to pray to Poseidon to help them sway his mind; and his response comes like an oracle of doom, though it wells up from a shattered heart. Hence the tension of Achilles' being: he is as incisive as he is overwrought, both clear and blurred with emotion, strung like a taut bow and yet breaking into sentences that impinge upon the even flow of thought and rhythm.

Power that exerts no deliberate control over others or even over himself, power that is an inner fire—such power is tantamount to passion, to intensity. And Achilles is intense. Look at Antilochus holding back his hand to prevent him from taking his own life after the loss of Patroclus. Look at Priam moving him to tears. Look at him in his bid to kill Agamemnon. Every experience is a total one. For him there is no mitigation, as if "the be-all and end-all" had to take place right here and now.

Any compromise or policy is thus alien to Achilles' nature. When he shifts position and allows Patroclus to go and help the routed Achaeans, it is not out of concern for their plight. What prompts him is love for his imploring friend, a love that takes the form of a shattering dream (*Il.* 16.97ff.):

Oh if it only could happen, / O Zeus and Athena and Apollo,
that not one of the Trojans / be saved as many as exist
and no, not one of the Greeks, / but the two of us be out of this doom,
so that alone we reduce / the sacred crown of Troy's walls.

For the same reason Achilles will not be bought back by Agamemnon's gifts; if he returns to fight, it can only be because of a greater passion than his initial wrath. And in book 19 (the book of the so-called reconciliation) is not his refusal to eat consistent with his character? Again, nothing else matters but the enveloping moment of grief and revenge. He makes light of Odysseus' advice as well as of reparations. In rejecting the communal meal, he seems to be living on another plane. That Athena should inject nectar into him to save him from famine shows him in a divine twilight—somewhere between the absolute present and approaching death.

Intense moments of characterization are actually realized in self-contained scenes: Achilles grows on us turn by turn, always the same and yet ever renewed. To find him most complete and self-composed we must look more closely at

Homer's final touch: the scene of Hector's ransom in the last book of the *Iliad* (24.468ff.).

The setting itself is significant. Achilles and his friends are not found engaged in any typical occupation (for example, banqueting or pouring libations), as Homer's characters normally are when being visited. The meal is over, friends are bustling around, and Achilles is caught in a casual moment. There is a sense of vacancy, a receptive atmosphere, as if all strain had spent itself.

Priam enters unseen, suddenly appearing before Achilles as a suppliant. There is wonder, silence; the sudden vision is all-absorbing: Achilles and the great old king face to face; opposing worlds suddenly made palpable in two human images. In that mighty pause all war seems at an end, dissolved in the light of a fresh perception, as when enemies look into each other's eyes and wonder at the discovery of a common innocence.

Speech, when it comes, is the inevitable voice of that mutual presence. "Think of your father, O Achilles," says Priam; and the focus naturally expands, image begets image: Priam is no different from Achilles' father, Peleus, and, from the same perspective, Hector is no different from Achilles himself or from Patroclus. The two men weep, each over their own woe, but their tears are universally significant. They weep, indeed, over an outraged world, over humanity as a whole.

A new spirit now stirs in Achilles, as he gently touches the old man, helps him rise, pities him, dwells upon life's sorrow, bewails his own doom, and with dismay recognizes himself as the ravager of Troy's once happy land. Is he a newborn sage? No, a savage nature still simmers beneath the temporary peace. When Priam insists on the speedy release of Hector's corpse, the earlier murderous hatred seizes

Achilles again; and, almost in fear of himself, in fear lest he lay a hand on the old man, he bounds from the room like a lion to propitiate Patroclus' ghost. That contact with the dead restores the disrupted moment, sets him again at peace. He has Hector laid on the bier and returns, telling the old man that his son is at last released to him.

And now Achilles achieves an even deeper serenity. He invites Priam to eat with him. "Even Niobe ate," he says, "after losing her wonderful children" (24.602ff.). He explains: she ate because she had to come to terms with life again, and only afterward, when transformed into a rock, did she gush— and eternally gushes—her tears down the mountain slope; for life has its brief moment, while the world's grief is unending. Here Achilles grows philosophical, looking at myth and reality in the light of one common experience, sensitive to the deep symbolism of an ancient tale.

That taking of food, that feeling of sparkling wine in the parched throat, that replenishment is like a rebirth. Things can be seen afresh. Achilles and Priam look at each other in silence. The beautiful features of the old man fill Achilles' vision. He is lost in high contemplative delight. To see here is to visualize; and vision is perception, understanding, intelligence, tenderness.

The hero is thus recomposed in the man. How significant that this final picture shows no mighty deed but a moment of sympathetic insight. The development appears both startling and inevitable—startling in that it runs counter to any conventional heroic pattern and is freshly realized at each point; inevitable in that it forcibly proceeds turn by turn from such simple concrete acts as touching, seeing, eating, drinking, as if each step were implicit in the logic of things. And it is also swift and full, in keeping with Achilles' powers of realization. For the truth comes to him suddenly, through the wonder of visual or sensuous perceptions, and not through long reflection or divine revelations passively received.

It follows, then, that we cannot take Achilles for granted or give him any one-sided attribute. "He is wanton, he is cruel, he has lost all sense and all shame," says Apollo after he has seen him maiming Hector's body (cp. *Il.* 24.41–45). "His senses are in him and wisdom and goodness; he will be tender and forbearing to a man that comes as his suppliant," says Zeus to Priam through Iris, enjoining him to go and ransom Hector's body (*Il.* 24.157–58). Both views are true; both are pertinent to a wild nature seeking within itself for the sources of its own humanization. Is Achilles baffling and unfathomable? Patroclus may be nearer the mark when, trying to move him to pity for the Achaeans, he cries out (*Il.* 16.29ff.):

> . . . we are helpless before you, O Achilles;
> oh never may such be mine / the wrath which within
>   you you foster,
> O man-of-dread-virtue . . .
> O pitiless, no, not to you / was the-horseman-Peleus a
>   father,
> no, nor Thetis your mother; / but the grey-gleaming
>   waves gave you birth
> and the precipitous cliffs, / so hard are the senses
>   within you.

The unique word *ainaretēs* ("of-dread-virtue") is evocative, joining as it does a sense of excellence with that of something strange, uncanny, sinister. It conveys the idea of an extraordinary being, magnificent and cruel like a god or a fact of nature, as distant as he is intimately present, as though the wild and familiar sea coursed through his veins.

No villain or ideal hero, does Achilles, then, stand beyond good and evil? Not that either. Rather, both good and evil brood powerfully within him, as if the very notion of them were being discovered. Here is the fierce pulse of growth. Opposing instincts wring the resisting mettle each in its own direction, and the individual self is wrought into form blow after blow.

Achilles' ambiguities are rooted in existence; they hark back to a logic that lies deeper than any narrow ethics might suppose. The same hand that delightfully plays the lyre in *Il.* 9.186 plundered that very lyre from Eetion's city, wreaking slaughter and destruction. Slaying Lycaon, he says in the same breath (*Il.* 21.106), "You also, O dear one, must die . . . since also Patroclus died." Pitying Priam yet feeling an instinct to kill him, he rushes from his presence.

Or let us look at the basic issues of life and death. Achilles is the only Homeric hero who yearns to die and actually seems inclined to suicide (*Il.* 18.33). Yet he is the greatest lover of life, whose shade in Hades says that it is better to be a poor man's slave than to be king of the dead. It is in the same spirit that he rejects Agamemnon's war (*Il.* 9.401ff.):

> Nothing is to me more than life, / not worth it are all the possessions
> which once Ilium possessed / the lovely-well-settled-city . . .
> not worth it is all that the threshold / of the far-shooting-god holds within,
> in the temple of Phoebus Apollo, / out in Pytho-the-rocky.
> They can surely be plundered / oxen and goodly sheep,
> they can surely be purchased / tripods and tawny horses;

but the life of a man / returns not—not to be plundered
nor to be seized when once / it passes out of one's lips.

What shall we make of such passages? Shall we conclude
that the hero is inconsistent? No, contradictions are there only
for those who judge externally, by categories. On the contrary,
we see a deep-seated consistency if only we stop positing a
heroic or moral code and look, rather, at the inner stress that
is productive of character. What matters is the tone, the mode
of being. It is indeed the distinction of Achilles that he shows
the same kind of intensity in the most disparate or opposing
attitudes, a persistency which, through the very process of
change, is ever more itself. Even his yearning to die and his
love of life are aspects of the same thing—a vitality so full-
blooded that, if balked of its boon, it can only find its proper
fulfillment in death.

Can we say, then, that Homer conceived such a character
deliberately? No. If anything, he had in mind the awesome
figurehead of a traditional hero. But at his touch the action
developed its own dynamic movement, and at its center the
hero was attuned to it, as if action were immediately converted into terms of experience and character. The very current of events appeared to run like a ferment through the
fibers of the man, removing him from habitual behavior and
touching off self-renewing capacities.

It will not do to object that events in the *Iliad* are predetermined and that Achilles must act accordingly. Rather, the
fatality of events is worked into the fatality of character and
vice versa. The two continually mold each other. What matters
is how convincing the truth of this relation—the impact, the
interplay, the nature of action and reaction—is.

Removed from the living text of the poems, Achilles has

lived a vicarious life—to anthropologists as a culture-hero, to literary historians as a typical epic hero, sublime, undaunted, wronged, and vindicated in the end. But, insofar as Homer is concerned, what really interests us is the fact that Achilles has seized the imagination of listeners and readers. If he does so, it is because he was so vitally realized in instance after instance; and this realization, we have seen, was brought about by focusing on self-contained dramatic moments.

Current scholarship, however, posits both a traditional hero and a traditional style without inquiring into any intrinsic reason. Thus, in connection with Achilles we have typical heroic themes such as the wrath theme or the theme of a hero mourning for his friend.

But why did such themes exist in the first place? Surely because they reflect crucial moments of life placed in their relevant setting. Rather than giving us a protracted narrative, the poet presents the character and the occasion all at once. The action centers around a figure, setting it in high relief at a certain spot and moment.

A theme, if there be any, is thus due to Homer's concreteness, and not the other way round. It points to a hero's actual position in the face of what is affecting him there and then. Hence the single powerful moments. Especially Achilles could hardly have been treated otherwise; his points of experience required all possible focus. The "Ransom of Hector's Body" (the last book of the *Iliad*) is a good example. It would be perverse to say that it results from an adaptation of such themes as "mutilation of a corpse," "mourning for a dead hero," "assembly in Olympus." This would be to ignore the imaginative impact that blended characters and action all at once. Surely what came first was the need to realize the event dramatically and thus to see it in its concrete manifestations, each of which had to have its pertinent setting. Human pas-

sions and divine influences converge. We have a moment of
decision that finds its points of focus in Troy, in Achilles' tent,
on Olympus. Conceived as it is, it could not have been treated
in straight narrative as a mere episode of Achilles' life or of
the Trojan War.

Even so, each appearance of Achilles creates its own
space and time, becoming a little self-enclosed drama that
summons into its sphere the participation of gods and men.
But, we may ask again, why the need to conceive in this way,
why this dramatization, this concreteness? Because each step
carries with it the full burden of a fateful moment. As Shakespeare puts it (*Julius Caesar*, 2.1.66–69):

> The Genius and the mortal instruments
> are then in council; and the state of man,
> like to a little kingdom, suffers then
> the nature of an insurrection.

V

Diomedes is similar to Achilles in being haunted by divine associations and then restored to a new sense of humanity. The goddess Athena loved his father Tydeus: she
would have made him immortal had she not seen him eating
the head of an enemy on the battlefield, whereupon she with-
drew in horror. Agrios (the name means "Savage") was his
uncle. A wild Thracian king, master of man-eating horses,
was his namesake, perhaps identical with him originally. As
Gilbert Murray remarks, mythology gives him an uncanny
background.

There is nothing of these legends in Homer; but a divine,
nonhuman aura surrounds Diomedes (cp. *Il.* 5.4–6). Athena,
infusing strength into him, repeatedly reminds him of Tydeus, as if she wished to give him that immortality which she

had to deny his father. He is, at her side, a peer of the gods, and yet, later, the most temperate among the Achaeans.

How did Homer achieve this effect? How did this human character in the making take its form? Again through concrete dramatic situations. Look at *Iliad* 5 and 6, the books in which Diomedes most distinctly appears. We first find him in man-to-man combats, strengthened by Athena's touch. But, significantly enough, the battlefield is at this point invaded by gods participating on both sides. What will he do, this over-powering son of Tydeus? Will he strike at man and god alike? And if not, how will he be able to distinguish between mortals and man-shaped gods? Athena grants him this power of recognition by removing from his eyes the cloud which obstructs his human sight; but she hardly mends matters when she tells him to keep away from all gods but Aphrodite.

The critical moment comes when Diomedes hits Aeneas with a huge stone that would have killed him had not Aphrodite, his mother, lifted him away, enveloping him in her robe. Diomedes now attacks Aphrodite, wounding her hand; the goddess cries out and is driven by Ares back to Olympus. And what of Aeneas? Dropped by his mother, he is rescued by Apollo. But Diomedes, driven on by his aroused impulse, pursues his attack even against Apollo (*Il.* 5.432ff.):

> And he leapt on Aeneas / Diomedes-good-at-the-war-cry
> knowing that over Aeneas / Apollo himself held his hand;
> but not even the great god / revered he; and ever was striving
> to kill Aeneas and from him / take away the wonderful arms.
> Three times then did he leap / in a rage to smite and to kill him;

three times at him struck the god, / on the shining
 shield struck Apollo.
But when indeed the fourth time / he rushed on
 Aeneas like a demon,
then with a dreadful cry / so spoke far-shooting Apollo:
"Oh beware, you son of Tydeus, / go backward, and
 with the gods
match yourself not in thought: / they can never be
 equal, the tribes
of the-gods-that-never-can-die / and of men-that-walk-
 down-on-earth.

At last Diomedes retreats. We find him later (793) alone
by his chariot, away from the battle, stanching the blood of a
wound. There Athena rushes upon him. "Ah, quite unlike
himself is the son whom Tydeus begot," she mocks, and in-
cites him this time against Ares, who is raging near by. We
now see the goddess and the hero side by side on the chariot;
she drives and directs his spear against the war-god who,
with a shattering roar, vanishes like a stormy cloud into the
sky.

In the next instance (*Il.* 6.119ff.), Diomedes appears as a
changed man. Confronting Glaucus (an ally of the Trojans),
he hesitates, wondering whether he is god or man. He who
previously attacked gods now refrains from attacking a man
in the belief that he might be a god. How can we explain this
change? And does it not contradict that power given him by
Athena to distinguish between gods and men?

We must try to understand the change in Diomedes by
looking at the way in which he develops as a character. What
Athena had given him was simply the power of outward dis-
crimination, which hardly affected his mounting spirits and
did not prevent him from actually coming to grips with gods.

A deeper, truer ability to distinguish is now required, one not prompted by any miracle but by introspection and thought. For a divine, mysterious quality pervades nature; and a man is no less than a god, a god no more than a man insofar as the essence of natural powers is concerned. Glaucus, an unknown being standing before Diomedes in the full prowess of his countenance, might well be a god in a world wherein gods love the human form. What is the difference, then? It is implicit in the Delphic "Know thyself," which contains a sense of limit, condition, form, dignity. A man, in other words, must look at human qualities in their intrinsic value and not confuse them with any sign of outward power or exemption from mortality and suffering.

Diomedes thus now discovers for himself the difference between gods and men. Pertinent to his question "who are you?" is the reply of Glaucus (*Il.* 6.145ff.):

> O great-hearted son of Tydeus, / why do you ask me my lineage?
> As generations of leaves / even such are men's generations.
> The leaves at one moment the wind / sheds down, but others the forest
> puts forth at blossoming time, / and the season of spring comes again.
> Even so men's generations: / one is born and the other fades out.

In stating that he is a man, Glaucus also explains the nature of man, as if he were interpreting for Diomedes Apollo's message: individual existence seen both in its glory and its transience. Even so a leaf has its high moment; but then the wind sweeps it down to earth to dissolve in the soil. And what does such an insight purport in regard to character? A si-

multaneous sense of power and measure. The grace of the
moment is one with a sense of transience. Its integrity would
be undermined by imputing to it superhuman powers.

Diomedes is thereafter as wise as he is brave (cp. *Il.*
9.32ff., 697ff.; 14.110ff.). He so speaks, for instance, to Agamemnon (*Il.* 9.698ff.): "If only you never had made any appeal to Achilles, offering numberless gifts. Proud he is at all
times; and now you have doubled his pride. . . . Well . . . let
him fight when he will. . . . Now we must eat, we must
drink . . . to-morrow we'll fight, we'll resist." Here is
strength, but tempered with resignation, patience, and
awareness of what is possible and what is impossible.

The characterization of Diomedes is still achieved
through the actuality of dramatic moments, but it is swifter,
less complex than in the case of Achilles. The startling change
in him within the same day comes from shocks sustained in
the field, while the intervening battle scenes give us an increased sense of time with their regular beat moment to moment. Each scene has a visual impact, as in a vase painting:
(1) Diomedes and Athena; (2) Diomedes against Aeneas and
Aphrodite; (3) Diomedes and Apollo; (4) Diomedes alone,
wounded; (5) Athena and Diomedes against Ares; (6)
Diomedes and Glaucus. Notice also the general setting: in
book 5 the battlefield is rife with gods; in book 6 the human
battle is left to itself, without gods. Homer works up the character of Diomedes by the simplest means: placing him face to
face with gods and with men.

Pure visualization is thus filled with significance; for the
opposing images are in themselves evocative. The issues of
mortality and immortality inevitably affect them, giving dramatic evidence to their tension and position. It is as if the
tragedy of Homer's heroic world here reached its climax: over-

bearing heroes ill at ease with their mortal weakness, gods participating at their sides in the moment of glory, the unavoidable crisis when the dividing line between them must be drawn.

Diomedes goes through this ordeal in his own way, first as an overwhelming figure with Athena fanning his primordial fire, then chastened into character. It is Apollo who is central to this process. The god's blows and words forge him anew as a man in spirit as well as species; hence the hero's restraint. Character, again, must here be understood in a fundamental way, in its etymological sense, as a carving out of primal matter rather than a sum of idiosyncrasies.

VI

Homer's concreteness inevitably hits on the truth of things. Just as it impinges on the mythical background, so does it penetrate and dilute any traditional incrustation. In these respects, the treatment of Agamemnon is no different from that of Achilles and Diomedes.

Agamemnon, supreme leader, king of golden Mycenae, might have been expected to be the most royal and the greatest of the Achaeans. But this is far from the case. Why? Because of the dramatic moment that opens the poem and influences the whole action.

The initial scenes of the *Iliad* are thus, in yet another respect, all-important; for we see the great king immediately entangled in the meshes of his own power. To the father, Chryses, asking to ransom his daughter Chryseis, Agamemnon replies (*Il.* 1.26ff.):

> Never, old man, by the ships / by the hollow ships let me find you,
> either loitering now / or hereafter coming again

lest they bring you no help / the fillet and staff of the
   god.
Her will I not release; / old age will sooner come on her
in the house that is ours, / in Argos, far from her home
plying the loom to and fro / and coming into my bed.
Away with you, do not provoke me, / that safely you
   may depart.

The arrival of Chryses instantly touches into action Agamemnon's temper, giving us an inkling of his character. We seem
to start from scratch. Though pertinent to the general subject
matter, the whole passage is self-contained; it could stand on
its own. We could understand it even if we ignored the rest
of the story. Agamemnon is summoned up afresh, whatever
role he might have played in pre-Homeric legend. For here
he asserts the victor's right, power of rank that does not know
how to yield, possessiveness, lust—whence the rebuff, the
outrage visited upon the priest and his god. And yet there is
no particular prejudice against Agamemnon. He is simply a
king clinging to his prerogative.

   Apollo's punishment, the plague, the seer's blame of
Agamemnon follow. A further step is taken. The king's power
is challenged, and his reaction is all the more wrenching (*Il.*
1.101ff.):

                                        . . . among them arose
   the hero-son-of-Atreus / Agamemnon-the-wide-ruling-
      king
   in anguish; and furious might / was in the dark depth
      of his midriff
   filling it up all round, / and his eyes were like flashing
      fire.

What will he do now? His reaction is typical. Afraid and

forced into submission by the god's evident punishment, he still has to vent his anger—not, indeed, on the god, but on the seer. "O prophet of evil," he cries out. And though he has to give up Chryseis, he will seize for himself another's prize.

Achilles stands up to Agamemnon, and yet another step is taken. The king's power is not only opposed, it is questioned, denied. He is driven to the brink, he must reassert his authority at all costs, and so he seizes Achilles' Briseis. He does so, as he tells Achilles (*Il.* 1.185ff.):

> . . . .that you may know
> how much stronger I am than you are / and others also
>   may shrink
> from speaking up as my equals / and matching
>   themselves in my sight.

Three scenes occur that place Agamemnon face to face with Chryses, Calchas, and Achilles, respectively. The last one leads to a climax; and so forceful is this representation act by act, such is the truth of the succeeding moments, that the characters emerge powerfully and convincingly out of the action itself. As the opposing images grow more definite, so do their respective positions and destinies. Their individual traits are deeply inscribed in the roles they will inevitably play.

Whereas Achilles withdraws and is driven to find within himself an inner power, Agamemnon exploits to the full what advantage is conventionally his own, gloats over it, and uses it up. Hence a weakness that is inherent in the very display of external power: when thwarted, he must retrieve his dwindling authority by any means—by insulting, threatening, making reprisals.

One might object that the facts of the story demand that Agamemnon's actions bring him woe, exposing his wrong.

But what matters is how such facts are realized and transformed into characterizing moments. Any flaw in the action is at once a flaw in Agamemnon himself, as if character developed and ran its course just as much as the events of the plot.

Why is Agamemnon particularly cruel and gruesome in the battle scenes (cp. Il. 11.101ff., 136ff., 146–47, 261; 6.53ff.)? It is because he is triumphant in these occasions; and, in keeping with his temper, he runs riot in the possession of power, in the wake of success. Why, on the other hand, is he the only hero who urges flight or withdrawal (cp. *Il.* 9.16ff., 14.74ff., cp. 2.139ff.)? Because when a reversal takes place he cannot face the struggle. Or, again, why is he so gratuitously abusive or blandly flattering when addressing one hero or the other when mustering his army (*Il.* 4.223ff.)? Because this is his way of exercising his power; he seems to relish a master's role in admonishing, instructing, blaming, praising.

Shall we say, then, that in Agamemnon Homer deliberately delineated a weak and impulsive man, a villain, or a tyrant? No, viewed generally, Agamemnon is cast in a heroic mold, like any other of the Homeric warriors—sanguine, warlike, proud. Look at him in the rally of the Achaeans (*Il.* 2.477ff.): his head and eyes are like those of Zeus, his waist like that of Ares, his chest like that of Poseidon. Or Priam sees him under the walls of Troy and exclaims (*Il.* 3.169f.), "Never my eyes saw a man of such beauty!" Or consider him fully armed before the combat (*Il.* 11.45f.) when "Hera and Athena thundered upon him, glorifying the king of golden Mycenae."

Homer gives to everything and everyone he portrays a natural fullness. Agamemnon is as vital a being as any. But in him this vital quality is a starting-point: it cannot be taken for granted; it has to be tested. And in Homer the sense of action or crisis is as strong as that of full-blooded individuals. Hence the imposing and yet precarious figure of a king. Is it, then, force of circumstance or his own temperament that makes Agamemnon what he is? The answer is unknowable. Let us simply say that Homer lets the happening strike its full note. He singles out the crucial point. All things here conspire to bring out regal power and its hollowness, summoning up the susceptibilities of a king.

We find, therefore, a lightness of touch in the characterization. There is no prejudice. No one characteristic is unduly pressed. Even at his worst, Agamemnon is anchored in the logic of experienced facts, however ruthless these may be. It is as though the nature of things were ever present in the representation itself: good and evil are seen as aspects of existence and not vice versa.

How to explain this unconstrained, natural objectivity? It comes, again, from the keen dramatization of the moment, which tends to throw into the background all a priori assumptions.

Homer's Agamemnon, therefore, is not the tragic figure of Greek drama. Whether the myths told about him by the tragedians are earlier or later than Homer, the Homeric treatment appears equally significant through comparison. If they are later, Homer provides the essential embryo; if earlier, Homer (even more significantly) sweeps away all superstructure. What stands out, in any case, is the pure immediacy of the moment.

For we find nothing in Homer of Iphigeneia's sacrifice, nothing of the horrific crimes that beset the house through the feud of Atreus and Thyestes. Agamemnon stands free before us, not caught in the trammels of an ancient fate but spurred by the anger of the occasion and his own instinct. It is not a family curse that crushes him, but the action itself, with its instantaneous sway.

Yet it is as though the tragic myth were made suddenly relevant. The ancient tale might seem to yield its overtones here, quite apart from any mythical setting. For divine wrath is at work both in tragedy and in Homer, except that in Homer cause and effect are much more immediate and fall within the same instant movement. Or look at the sense of fate. In Homer, it is just a foreboding quite merged with an irresistible impulse, while in tragedy it has an eschatological significance.

See also how much is intimated by a solitary Homeric flash. "Her will I not release," cries out Agamemnon about Chryseis, and, "I prefer her to my wedded wife, Clytaemnestra" (*Il*. 1.23 and 113). Do not such words evoke Cassandra and Clytaemnestra's bloody revenge?

Or consider how later, looking back, Agamemnon blames Ate, or Delusion, singling out this goddess as the special cause of his outrage (*Il*. 19.91ff.). But who exactly is Ate? She is temptation, a momentary distraction and blindness of the senses, a personification so transparent in Homer that the very word comes to denote a personal experience: "I was struck with *ate*." Here is a subtle, penetrating influence, almost identical with a wayward inner motion of the mind. And although Agamemnon also mentions "Zeus and the Moira and the dark-walking Erinys" (87), he does so desultorily, dismissing them, as if giving us a fleeting glimpse of those overpowering agencies which hold sway in the myths of Greek tragedy. Agamemnon dwells at length upon a different power—less obscure, more intimate and pervasive, near at hand. In portraying the familiar Ate, he seems to portray himself, revealing the brittleness of the strongest will, indulging in self-pity and thus exposing another strain of his character.

VII

Morals as well as myth or history are deeply affected by Homer's concreteness. Ideas concerning the relations between men and women are a case in point. We hardly find any preconceptions in Homer; most notably, he stands in contrast to the antifeminist strain which may be traced back to Hesiod. One reason for this is that women, like men, are rendered in the immediacy of their presence; and the direct portrayal of succeeding acts tends to oust any accessory or irrelevant qualification. Hence a spontaneous, untrammeled sense of truth.

A case in point is Helen. An evil genius in Aeschylus, a redeemed heroine in Euripides, an image of wickedness in Alcaeus, a eulogistic theme in Gorgias, a divinity in non-Homeric myths, she became a varied symbol throughout the ages; but in Homer she is quite human, a woman shown at crucial junctures of life.

It is in *Iliad* 3 that she is most conspicuous. We first find her in *Il.* 3.121ff.:

Iris to Helen came, / to Helen-white-armed, with a
   message

. . . .

and in the hall she found her, / there a great web was
   she weaving
purple-dyed, double-folded, / setting in it the many
   struggles
which the horse-taming Trojans / and the bronze-clad
   Achaeans
suffered for her own sake / at the hands of Ares in war.

Here concreteness attains its fullest scope: what is more real or typical than a woman weaving, and yet what more significant than this specific detail? For Helen is embroidering nothing less than the struggles being endured for her sake. The effect is as simple as it is stunning: in purely visual terms, the woman is set face to face with the fate that besets her. Her thoughts, we may imagine, are at one with the picture she is composing. But what are her feelings? Is she sad, repentant, proud? We are not told. Any utterance would be out of place, undermining the solemn moment, the rare, delicate touch that simultaneously calls up Helen and a whole world fallen under her spell. Here is a sudden realization of what she is. The work at the loom mirrors her life.

In the next scene, Helen, summoned by Iris, walks out to watch from the walls of Troy the Trojans and Achaeans temporarily at peace to make time for the hand-to-hand combat between Paris and Menelaus (*Il.* 3.139ff.):

> So having spoken, the goddess / put into her soul a
>   sweet longing
> for the husband previously hers / and for her city, her
>   parents.
> And at once veiling herself / in the white-gleaming
>   folds of her robe,
> out of the chamber she paced, / many a full tear
>   dropping down—
> not alone, at her sides / two attending women came
>   after,
>
> . . . .
>   And there
> were seated the city's elders, / hard by the West gates
>   of Troy,
> through old age now from the war / discharged, and
>   yet notwithstanding
> keen speakers like to cicadas / that in the woodlands
>   abiding

> from upon the branch of a tree / pour out their
>   blossoming voice;
> even such were the elders of Troy / as at the wall they
>   were sitting.
> And when before them they saw / Helen walking up to
>   the tower,
> softly to one another / wingéd words they so talked:
> "No shame it is to the Trojans / and to the well-greaved
>   Achaeans
> for such a woman's sake / to suffer a long-lasting pain.
> Strangely like an immortal, / a goddess, she is in her
>   looks.
> Yet even though she be so, / let her go back in the
>   ships—
> away from us, from our children, / not here to bring
>   future woe."

Again we are given a picture of Helen rather than hearing her or being told about her, but the tears make her image more telling, more particularly significant. She is simply longing for her past; and any further characterization would detract from the wonder and significance of this fleeting vision.

Then Helen passes before the elders of Troy. Our visual impression now becomes their own. The moment of visualization is thus singled out in itself and by itself; it is both perception and thought. The elders see and speak. They speak softly, secretly, as though voicing an inner conviction too true, too shattering to be spoken aloud. They say it is no shame to die for Helen. For hers is beauty in a supreme sense—a divine effluence shed upon the world, a thing of the gods.

That the elders should so feel and speak certainly explains Helen to us: what she is, what she appears to be. They fully express her beauty through what they say. And yet Lessing's contention that we see here the essential difference between poetry and the visual arts only gives us a partial insight. For great painting and sculpture as well as poetry transcend all nicety of detail; and in this passage what gives resonance to the words of the elders is the fact that Helen is so visually effective, as if Homer were drawing rather than narrating. She is central to the scene, so vitally realized as an image that she dynamically brings the elders within the compass of her presence. So in a sculptural group one figure exerts its spell over the others, or all over one another, and a dramatic relation is thus made palpable. What matters is the form itself, its existence, its resilience, its basic innocence precluding all narrow judgment. The sympathetic response of the elders is no less than this. Who can blame Helen? Yet who can justify or praise her? She is as real as she is unfathomable. The reader participates in the wonder.

In the following scene Priam calls Helen to the ramparts (*Il.* 3.162ff.):

> Hither before me now come, / dear child, and sit at my side,
> to look at your husband of yore / and at your kinsmen and friends.
> In nothing you are guilty to me, / it is the gods that are guilty
> who launched upon me this war / this tearful war of the Achaeans.
>
> . . . .
>
> And to him did she answer / Helen-divine-among-women:
> "Awe is mine here before you, / awe, o dear father, and fear.

> Would that death had then pleased me / ah, cruel death
>   on the day
> when hither I followed your son / leaving my home and
>   my kinsmen
> and my one daughter beloved / and the sweet friends
>   of my youth.
> But these things did not happen, / wherefore I am
>   wasted in tears.

Helen, up to now so self-contained, here breaks out of her silent mold. Vivid juxtaposition, face-to-face presence inevitably turn to dialogue. But why are the words so powerful? Because, as spontaneously as in a greeting, they arise from the pure encounter and yet also express what these persons are in each other's eyes. Priam's vision is closer, more intimate than that of the elders, and Helen cannot but respond. Rather than merely speaking or conversing, they suddenly stand mutually revealed. The words are like an articulation of the respective images.

And Helen now grows more familiar. Her innocence is more explicitly recognized, and, in Priam, judgment blends with contemplative wonder. But what of her response to him? She is overwhelmed, much more so than if she had been accused. We may compare this to what she says to Hector later (*Il.* 6.343ff.):

> O brother of mine in my shame, / in the chilling woes I
>   contrived,
> would that upon that day / when first my mother begot
>   me
> there had come to carry me away / some dreadful blast
>   of the winds
> dashing me into the mountains / or waves of the wide-
>   roaring sea,

> even there blotted out / before these things ever
>   were. . . .

How significant it is that no blame is cast on Helen by others, only by herself. Her image thus becomes more real through its own force—still solidly present, still a full visual form, still self-contained, but acquiring an inner depth that projects her beyond the occasion and lets us see her as a character removed from time and place.

How should we interpret Helen's self-recrimination? Is it repentance, remorse, self-pity? No, none of these. Rather, it is a haunting sorrow for what happened or did not happen— a feeling baffling to anyone, but most baffling and dreadful to the one who is directly involved. Helen's tears are for what has been denied her rather than the expression of an afflicted conscience craving, perhaps, for forgiveness. She does not ask to be forgiven, nor does she seek any extenuation. On the contrary, she plunges right into the thick of the surrounding woe. Her grief is as inevitable as her fate.

Fatalism then? No, not fatalism either. For fatalism brings resignation and lack of tension, while there is passion in Helen. Her whole personality is stirred to utterance. Though she says "it did not happen," though she recognizes the ineluctability of events, her cry rises full and clear against the ruins. That cry, at least, is not determined by any god or fate. Although it cannot change the order of things, it carries with it, as in a flash, the sense of all her frustrated hopes and joys and is thus a vindication of herself. Helen retains the dignity of her pain, whatever may have happened. Hence, even at this low ebb, the pure high relief of her image.

In the sequel to the above scene, Helen identifies for Priam the Achaean heroes below the walls. But she cannot see her brothers and says (*Il*. 3.234ff.):

> Now all the others I see / the other bright-eyed
>   Achaeans
> whom I could recognize, / whose names I surely could
>   tell;
> but there are two whom I see not; / where are they?
>   Two leaders of men
> Castor-the-tamer-of-horses / and Pollux-good-with-his-
>   fists,
> brothers truly my own / to whom the same mother
>   gave birth.
> Either they came not hither / from Lakedaimon-the-
>   lovely
> or they indeed came hither / upon the sea-faring ships,
> and yet they are now unwilling / to enter the battle of
>   men
> in their fear of the shames / and reproaches that greatly
>   beset me.

Here again, Helen is revealed through a visual relation: as previously face-to-face with Priam, so now in sight of the Achaean host. Anguish thus yields for a while to a bright, colorful view, as her wandering gaze blends the past with the vivid present now opening before her. But there is a sinister gap: her brothers are not there. Is it because they are ashamed of her? That gap lets in pain again.

Some scholars would here point to an effect of "shame culture" rather than "guilt culture." But we may, rather, take into account Homer's objectivity. As she has before, Helen is grieving in light of what has happened or failed to happen— grieving over herself, on whose account there is a war that might turn a brother's love to hatred. She feels no contrition but a shattering realization of what is. Introspection is made part and parcel of objective vision.

What follows in the story is the fight between Paris and
Menelaus, Paris rescued by Aphrodite and wafted back to his
chamber. At this point the goddess comes to Helen upon the
ramparts (*Il.* 3.383ff.):

> she found her
> upon the rampart up high, / and around her the
>   women of Troy.
> Her hand on the fragrant robe, / she seized upon it and
>   shook it.
> In an old woman's shape, / sore-ridden with years, did
>   she speak;
> a spinner of wool who for Helen / when in Sparta she
>   lived long ago
> used to make beautiful things, / a woman by her most
>   beloved.
> In her likeness, to Helen / divine Aphrodite thus spoke:
> "Come hither; it is Alexander / that calls you to come to
>   the house.
> There he is in his chamber, / there on the well-inlaid
>   bedstead.
> Radiant he is with his beauty / and his robes; you
>   never would say
> that after fighting a man / there he came, but rather to
>   a dance
> he was going, or from a dance / now resting there was
>   he sitting."
> So she spoke, and her heart / she set astir in its depth.
> And when Helen perceived / the beautiful neck of the
>   goddess
> and the charm of her breasts, / the shining light of her
>   eyes,
> with wonder then was she stricken, / words welled up
>   and she called:

"Ah fatal goddess, why now / why do you long to
   deceive me?

Now indeed further afield / in the world of fair-sited
   cities

you'll lead me on—either Phrygia / or the lovely land of
   Maeonia

if even there is now living, / out of mankind, a man
   that you love.

Now indeed because Menelaus / overcame divine
   Alexander

and wishes—ah, for my shame— / to take me back to
   his home,

is this why you now hither / have come to me weaving
   wiles?

Go then and sit by his side, / withdraw from the path
   of the gods

and never again with your feet / to Olympus tread back
   your way,

but ever attending upon him / take pains and ever
   safeguard him,

until he will make you his wife, / his wife or even his
   slave.

Thither I will not go / —anger it would stir all around—

thither attending his bed, / the women of Troy will in
   future

cast on me their reproach, / there's measureless grief in
   my soul."

Then, to her, full of anger / replied divine Aphrodite:

"O wrangler, do not provoke me / lest in anger I leave
   you

and I so utterly hate you / as now I wondrously loved
   you

and between the two sides / a dreadful feud I devise,

> there, between Argives and Trojans / and in cruel
>   doom you might die."
> So she said, and she shuddered / Helen-the-Zeus-
>   begotten.
> She went enclosing herself / in the gleaming white of
>   her robe,
> silent, unseen by the women, / the goddess' power
>   upon her.

Just as Helen had been summoned by Iris to the ramparts, so she is now summoned by Aphrodite to Paris' chamber—faced first with her woe, then with her love. Again, as always, we see movement, encounter, position. Confrontation precipitates the mental process.

Especially in this scene, what matters is the sudden realization of the images, the penumbra of suggestion that surrounds them, the resonance of what is said. Why does Aphrodite first appear to Helen as an old woman known long ago? Because Helen's present absorbs her past. And why is Paris presented in all his charm, as if were going to a dance or had just stopped dancing? Because that was how he must have appeared to her in Sparta when he first visited and took her away. Homer's style is to concentrate experience, both past and present, into one concrete moment. Powerfully, though perhaps unwittingly on Homer's part, the actual instant swells into a mirage, gathering the past into a specious present.

Helen is thus deeply stirred; and she is stunned when she recognizes Aphrodite's features in the old woman. Why this second transformation? Because, again, deeper levels of reality rise to the surface. It is as if Helen were witnessing once more the very emergence of love through the ways of ordinary life implicitly embodied in the familiar old woman.

That vision of beauty is like an image of herself. It is the bewitching spell which she exerts and which, in turn, destroys her. Her own life is mirrored in what she sees.

Considered in this light, Helen's address to Aphrodite almost reads like a soliloquy. In place of the goddess, we might understand her own heart. Here is the eternal temptation, dream, illusion—an irresistible force drawing a woman away from home and country. And here also is the feeble resistance opposed to this force—fear of what others will say and the attending anguish.

But Aphrodite is no figment of the brain. There she stands, supreme, imperious. She will brook no compromise, no delay. A divine power is undoubtedly at work. It drives Helen to Paris; and she goes, veiling herself, unseen, just as she did when leaving Sparta long ago.

In the ensuing scene, the same immediate, tense outline delineates Helen face-to-face with Paris. She sits before him turning aside her eyes and yet speaks: "You came away from the battle; ah if only there you had died," and then a moment later says, "But no, do not fight again . . . lest you die." This is a swift transition from hatred and rage to renewed self-surrender. Aphrodite works, as it were, from within; the rekindled love replaces all longing for Menelaus, and Paris again seduces her (*Il.* 3.441ff.):

> "But come now, in love's delight / down in the bed let us lie.
> For no, never as now / has love so encompassed my mind,
> not even when the first time / from Lakedaimon-the-lovely
> I took you and sailed away / upon the sea-faring ships,
> and in the island of Cranae / with you I mingled in love;

> more than then I do love you / and a sweet yearning
> besets me."
> So said he, and led the way, / the woman followed his
> steps.

Time after time, Helen's image grows before us, and so
strongly that she is finally impressed upon our minds as character quite apart from any particular passage.

For such a realization to be possible, the hero or heroine
must be solidly present as a figure. The physical dimension
keeps the fluid mental world in focus. On the other hand,
only basic states of mind are capable of so permeating the
figure as to turn it into a haunting image, a character. The
impact is thus simple and immediate. What produces the impact is fullness of the figure's response to a crucial situation—
a response which is tantamount to a role or destiny, to character in a most vital sense.

In such a style there is little room for pointed or narrow
characterization. The very suspicion of it would be out of
place. No one could say that Helen is vain because she weaves
into her web struggles endured by others for her sake. Likewise, it would be misguided to impute self-pity to her
wrenching cry. Even more, it would be wrong to take her as
a sensualist or wanton. As she weaves, her silent image implies consciousness, not self-consciousness: thought itself face
to face with reality. When she erupts into self-recrimination,
it is a result of shattering inner pain for all that has happened.
When she yields again to Paris, it is no sensual pleasure but,
rather, the overpowering force which Aphrodite embodies.
So, every time we see Helen, her image stands out strong and
clear before our eyes—whether pensive, afflicted, or flushed
with shame and passion. Any detailing would blur the perfect
contours, just as any physical description of her beauty would
have a belittling effect.

True as this roundedness is of all Homer's characters, it is especially striking in Helen, exposed as she is to moral strictures. Elemental conditions are embodied in her—conditions that might be regarded as negative because of their destructive consequences and yet so vitally rooted in the nature of things that they give us pause and fill us with wonder. This is why, in Homer, it is Paris, light-hearted adventurer, who gets the blame, not Helen. But not even Paris can be made into a villain, belonging as he does to Helen's sphere.

VIII

The contrast between the Homeric and the post-Homeric fortune of a character is a very revealing one. To Helen we may compare Odysseus. In Pindar and the Greek tragedians (as well as in later literature) he became the very embodiment of unscrupulous craftiness, while in Homer this craftiness is only a minor aspect of his rich and versatile nature.

Once again Homer's concreteness deeply affects the moral view of character. Odysseus in the *Odyssey* is shown for what he is by the friction of events as they unfold instance after instance. What characterizes him are the instincts and capacities awakened by the strenuous effort of his return home, not by any preconceived portrait or pattern of behavior. Thus, each occasion or situation elicits a new response: among the Lotus-eaters he must be resolute and spurn the sweet temptation of the lotus fruit; in the cave of the Cyclops he must use all his craft and wit to escape; with Aeolus he is a desperate suppliant; with the Laestrygonians, a cool-headed fugitive in the general rout; with Circe, a breaker of spells, a lover, and a genial guest; at the entrance of Hades, a passionate or sympathetic communer with ghosts; with the Sirens, a charmed listener contriving to escape from their spell; between Scylla and Charybdis, a skipper on the edge of death;

in Thrinacia, a wise leader disappointed by his men; with
Calypso, again, a lover and a dreamer after home. Once back
in Ithaca, Odysseus must again test many of the same qualities before regaining his wife and kingdom.

The concreteness of Homer's treatment hardly leaves
room for any one-sided qualification. Just as actions or situations are many and varied, so are the strains of character.
Were we to trace Odysseus' qualities to one common source,
we should have to look for it in the sheer vitality of his nature—his instinct to survive, to live, to be free. Here is craftiness; but because it is a way to safety or recovery, it becomes
skill, ingenuity, inventiveness. Odysseus has wisdom; but it
is a feeling for relativity in the human condition and therefore
also a knowledge of how to deal with people and things.

In Odysseus, it is as if we witnessed the growth of in-
tellect from the very sap of life. For, on occasion, this wisdom
married to craft may breed thoughtfulness and reflection.
Similarly, Odysseus' inquisitiveness in new lands, or his
search for the points of the compass, might be seen as science
in the making; Dante singled it out when he had Odysseus
lead his men to an ultimate quest of the world's uninhabited
regions. Poetry, too, or the mastery of words, here finds its
place. For Odysseus, in order to win the Phaeacians and others to his cause, must tell his tale as well as he can; and they
are charmed as if listening to a poet (cp. *Od.* 11.368ff.). But
in Homer no ideal pursuit is ever abstracted from the basic
need that prompted it in the first place. Even while showing
the broadest qualities of mind, Odysseus is driven by the spur
of the occasion. What he does is to meet a pressing moment;
but such a moment is always so relevant to the general issues
of life that it rises above any immediate connection and seems
to tap unsuspected potentialities. Practical self-exertion thus
turns to introspection, thought, and imagination.

Take, for instance, Odysseus facing Nausicaa (*Od.*
6.141ff.):

> and Odysseus then wavered
> whether to cling at her knees / and so beg the beautiful
>   girl
> or just so, with words only, / sweetly, but from afar
> pray her that she might show him / the town and give
>   him clothes.
> So was he rapt in thought, / and it seemed to him the
>   best thing
> to beg her so with words only, / sweetly, but from afar
> lest, if he clasped her knees, / the girl be angry in her
>   heart.
> At once then with sweet words, / and yet with guile he
>   thus spoke:
> "I am your suppliant, o queen; / are you a goddess or
>   mortal?
> If you are one of the gods / that dwell in the spaces of
>   heaven,
> Artemis surely you are, / the daughter of Zeus-the-
>   great-god,
> like her in size and in looks, / like her in form I do
>   deem you.
> But if you are one of the mortals / who upon the earth
>   have their dwelling,
> thrice for you are they blesséd— / your father and
>   stately mother
> and thrice blesséd your brothers; / surely the spirit
>   within them
> always in new delight / must melt away for your sake
> as they see you as you are, / a blossom, going to the
>   dance.

But he in his inmost heart / happiest by far above all

who, prevailing with gifts, / should take you as wife to
his home.

For never yet such a being / I have ever seen with my
eyes,

neither any woman nor man, / wonder besets me as I
look.

In Delos once such a thing, / close by the altar of
Apollo,

the young shoot of a palm tree / soaring up high did I
see

(for even there have I been / and a great host was there
with me

upon that journey which brought me / a future of pain
and of woe).

Even such was that sight, / and a wonder so filled my
heart

long-lasting; for such a tree / never grew elsewhere on
earth.

Thus at you, o woman, I wonder, / in awe do I stand
and great fear

of laying hands on your knees; / a grievous pain is
upon me.

Yesterday, twenty days after, / I escaped from the wine-
colored sea

and up to then ever by waves / was I borne and
violence of storms

away from the isle of Ogygia; / now hither a god cast
me out,

so that perhaps even here / I may suffer further; I think
not

that any rest shall be mine; / no, much more grief is in
store.

But, O queen, do take pity; / through toil after toil it is
  you
whom I first have approached, / none other there is
  that I know
amongst the people who dwell / throughout the land
  and the city.
Oh, but show me the town / and give me a rag to
  throw round me,
or any wrapping or cloth / which you may have with
  you here.
And upon you may the gods / bestow all the things
  that you long for.
A man and a home withal / and concord of minds may
  they grant—
O blessing; for there is nothing, / nothing greater, more
  precious
than when feeling at peace / with thoughts attuned
  they hold house
a man and a woman. . . ."

As we read this speech, we can hardly ignore how pregnant is the juxtaposition of images—Odysseus and Nausicaa
facing each other. Sentiments, thoughts, and ideas are thus
held in focus and, however broad their range, are bound by
inevitable connection.

Here is a man shipwrecked, naked, and stranded on a
solitary shore. He sees a girl. Who is she? Will she help him?
How should he approach her? Delicacy, caution, and cunning
are immediately required. Odysseus rises to the occasion. He
is hungry and alone; and the sheer instinct to survive activates
his capacities. It is as if the moment and the place conspired
to make his character what it is.

And now the girl appears in all her beauty. His initial

cunning, the flattery of comparing her to Artemis, is soon cast aside. Odysseus dwells upon her human beauty; and, as he does so, the aesthetic sense prevails over all else. He is no longer crafty, but rapt in admiration and wonder. There is no praise, here, of any one detail or alleged quality: beauty is conjured up, as elsewhere in Homer, by the imagined joy of the beholder. And the visual sense now reigns supreme. It seems to supplant distress. It evokes thoughts of love, marriage, and the fullest joys of life.

As the feeling for beauty grows purer, more refined, Odysseus compares Nausicaa to the palm-tree in Delos. We are reminded of the *korai*, those figures of early Greek art whose enrobed trunk has the pure solidity of a column or a palm's stem. Aesthetic values are thus caught at their root. They are prompted by the sense of life and human loveliness, which, in its turn, had been brought home to Odysseus under the stress of necessity.

The tree of Delos also suggests the occasion on which Odysseus was there: the Trojan expedition and its subsequent miseries. Hence his woe, his need for help. "May the gods grant you whatever you long for," he says to Nausicaa, the usual blessing bestowed by a beggar upon anyone who gives him something, we might say. But Odysseus gives substance to the wish by stating so fully yet concisely in what the happiness of man and woman consists. And here is wisdom reaching beyond the occasion. The idea itself might seem commonplace if taken as an abstract maxim, but it escapes being so because it is so freshly prompted by the girl whose beauty makes him think of a bridegroom's joy—and perhaps also because the forsaken wanderer can see here the tantalizing shadow of his own happiness.

We may still wonder about Odysseus. Can this sensitive

admirer of Nausicaa be the same man who blinded the Cyclops? Can this sacker of cities be the same man whose mother
died missing his "gentleness of mind" (*Od.* 11.203)? Not only
the greatest variety of skills, but also of inner dispositions
and attitudes is embodied in his nature. Is this possible? No
combination of virtues can be plausibly attributed to a hero
by simply presenting him so.

How is it, then, that Homer's Odysseus is so convincing
as a real character? It is because he is so focal an image,
because of the light shed upon him from situation to situation.
What makes a character is not a set of qualities logically related to one another in an abstract way, but the fact that any
one quality is suddenly made manifest in a living shape. This
is so even in ordinary life. How often we find in someone we
know an unexpected capacity; and all at once it makes sense,
because this newfound capacity is immediately absorbed into
the vital presence of the person we know, and nature presents
us with a new perspective, our ordinary abstract logic giving
way to a deeper logic that we must build anew.

So it is with Odysseus. Light is thrown upon him continually from many sides. Through the first four books of the
Odyssey he is an image of the minds of others: that "man-of-
many-turns" sung by the Muse, the theme of Penelope's
dreams, the stimulus of Telemachus' thoughts, a threatening
cloud to the suitors, a haunting concern for Athena. We first
see him in flesh and blood sitting on the shore of Calypso's
island longing for Ithaca (*Od.* 5.151), and thence from day to
day in a swift succession of instances that impress his image
more and more firmly in our minds: in the act of building his
raft, in the act of sailing, in the act of a desperate swimmer
at last touching land, and so forth, up to his final day back
in Ithaca. Remembered, longed for, feared, seen, encountered, admired, welcomed or rejected, disguised or recog-

nized, faced by friend or foe. Odysseus stands at the center of the surrounding world, his presence magnified by those who look at him directly as well as by those who are thinking of him from afar. And his image thus grows solid, vitally relevant, appealing, intimate, and capable of absorbing into itself numberless and unnamed strands of experience.

The brightest instance of this image-making power occurs when Odysseus tells his story to the Phaeacians. They are spellbound as they watch and listen, as they see that the character who emerges from the story corresponds to the actual speaker.

How is this effect achieved and why does it come so simply and powerfully? One reason is that Odysseus' account never becomes a mere narrative. His wanderings, which lasted three years, are condensed into self-contained scenes enacted before our eyes, each time setting Odysseus in high relief over and above his anonymous crew—not because of any vainglory, but in order to render strongly and clearly the truth of the event itself. Whether we see him landing or sailing, whether addressing Circe or the Cyclops, he is silhouetted against the vast background of earth, air, and sea, each scene so circumscribed as to be readily visualized, as in a vase-painting, gathered around the image of one man. And the image so conjured up inevitably reflects on the speaker. The effect is thus quite different, say, from that of Aeneas telling Dido about the fall of Troy and the flight of his people. What strikes us here is the sharp contour. However complex, the individual ordeal is kept in focus. At the center stands the man himself.

"What are your thoughts?" says Arete to the listening Phaeacians at one point. "Here he is right before you, here is his shape, here his size" (*Od.* 11.336). It is as though the past moments of Odysseus' tale run into the present and find a locus in his image, which thus brightens to the eyes of all. We find a similar effect in Eurycleia's recognition (*Od.* 19.381ff.): the man she knew twenty years before suddenly peers through the present image. Indeed, the whole poem is so composed as to foster in Odysseus this magnetic appeal: strands of time, the glory of experience are made palpable by his presence.

No wonder, then, that he is convincing as a character. Like Arete, we might say that Odysseus is right there before us, living proof of what he recounts and of what he is thought to be.

No other Homeric character remains so persistently in focus as Odysseus. It is therefore no wonder that he alone has epithets which are perfectly pertinent to his role: "of-many-turns," "of many devices," and "much-suffering." His was an ingenuity that enabled him to escape from many ordeals; and, matched to this, he had strength to resist and endure, the capacity to suffer.

These qualities are bound together, in the *Odyssey,* by the strain of necessity, by the imperious instinct to live and find safety, as when, approaching Scheria, for two nights and days he resists the surging seas and then thoughtfully finds a landing spot where he will not be dashed against the cliffs.

But this blending of resourcefulness and endurance can be seen in broader terms. It is not confined to particular circumstances and narrow escapes. It takes its place and time in the larger movement of Odysseus' days. It becomes depth of experience and knowledge through suffering.

This view of Odysseus is voiced right at the beginning of the *Odyssey*: "of many men he saw the cities and knew their mind, and at sea great grief in his heart did he suffer, trying to save his own life and win the return of his friends." And

it is grief which is most naturally his great theme when, quite
apart from any particular exploit, he gives an essential account of himself (cp. *Od.* 5.222; 6.169; 7.24, 147, 152, 208, etc.).
Here is grief for lost friends, grief for calamities endured, grief
for life ebbing away and for a boon always slipping away; but
here also is grief that engenders endurance, strength, hope.
And even if the ultimate goal is elusive, there is still the joy
of again touching land; there is calm and replenishment after
the storm; there is a persistent taste for life, the sweet made
sweeter by its bitter counterpart. On this higher plane, resourcefulness becomes the capacity to learn and understand
the ways of life; and patience or endurance becomes thoughtfulness, reflection on the truth of things. Hence the wisdom
of a man sobered by experience, sad but resilient, as when
he tells Antinous (*Od.* 18.130ff.):

> Nothing weaker exists, / nourished by earth, than a
>   man,
> nothing amongst all creatures / that breathe and move
>   on the ground.
> Sure he is he will never / suffer any ill on the morrow,
> while the gods give him strength / and nimbleness is in
>   his knees;
> but when woes come upon him / which the blesséd
>   gods bring about,
> he yet bears them unwilling, / but with patience of
>   heart.
> Such is by nature the mind / of mortals-that-live-on-the-
>   earth,
> as the day cast upon them / by the father of gods and
>   of men.

This is the kind of life Odysseus himself has lived through;

and yet it is the life he chooses for himself when he refuses
Calypso's offer of immortality, saying (*Od.* 5.215ff.):

> O great goddess, ah no; / resent it not, I do know
> all you say: how below you / wise Penelope ranks. . . .
> But even so it is my will, / my yearning ever and ever
> to set foot in my home / and see the day of my return.
> Even if any god crush me / out in the wine-colored sea,
> I will endure having with me / the grief-bearing soul in
>   my breast.
> Great and many in the past / have been my woes and
>   my toils
> out in the waves and at war; / let this also happen
>   besides.

To Alcinous, who thinks Odysseus might be a god, he says
(*Od.* 7.208ff.):

> Alcinous, oh think it not / in your mind; I do not at all
> bear any resemblance to gods / who inhabit the spaces
>   of heaven,
> not in body nor form, / but to mortal men I resemble;
> to those amongst all that you know / who are most
>   afflicted with pain—
> to them alone of all men / I would liken myself for my
>   griefs.

Odysseus thus disowns all connection with the gods, he af-
firms his identity as a man; and he does so with zest, as if he
were once again refusing to exchange his mortal pain for any
gift of immortal bliss. Let Calypso and Circe pursue their even
lives of endless happiness in regions where no tension can
exist, no overriding issue can emerge. The life of a man must
be different. It is the days of grief and joy which make it what

it is and give it its intrinsic worth. Odysseus' restless spirit
could not have it otherwise.

Nor is this mortal state simply a condition of fact; it is an
intense feeling in all the affections. This inwardness is best
expressed by Odysseus when he tells the Phaeacians how he
encountered his mother's ghost at the entrance of Hades (*Od.*
11.204ff.):

> . . . there was I / in my mind debating and
>   wishing
> to embrace there the soul / of my mother now dead.
> Thrice I sprang up towards her, / to clasp her my spirit
>   commanded,
> thrice away from my arms, / like to a shadow or a
>   dream
> she flew, while in me the pain / grew sharper deep in
>   my heart,
> and at once speaking out / I said to her wingéd words:
> "O mother, why do you not / stay here for me yearning
>   to clasp you,
> so that even in Hades, / throwing round each other our
>   arms,
> we both may find fulfilment / in the cruel pleasure of
>   tears?
> Or is this but a phantom / which Persephoneia divine
> sped hither to make even greater / the throbbing pulse
>   of my pain?

Love, grief, and death are the sources of one vital passion.
What else is life about?

Here character is rooted in a sense of values. Through
Odysseus, Homer vindicates, in his own way, the dignity and
value of grief—what Aeschylus did in the *Agamemnon*, what
Sophocles did in *Oedipus at Colonus*, what Plato and Aristotle

failed to do. But Homer's Odysseus does so without any abstract statement of principles or any special piety to help him; he does so through his sheer capacity to live, to endure, to play his role to the end.

Yet Odysseus' qualities are godlike. An unusual glory surrounds him, and it contrasts with his frail human frame. The Cyclops, who had heard prophecies about his arrival, is surprised to see before him such a small, insignificant-looking man. Circe is similarly surprised. There is a wonder about him that transcends his person and sometimes even transfigures him in the eyes of those who see him.

As if to highlight this divine element, Athena constantly appears at the side of Odysseus or works from a distance, furthering his cause. At the beginning of the *Odyssey*, she stimulates Telemachus' thoughts of his father, instilling him with the Odyssean spirit. Then, among the Phaeacians, and even more so back in Ithaca, she continually advises, warns, and encourages Odysseus. But Athena's help is never external. It is not that of a god who miraculously paves the way and smooths away difficulties; she participates in his efforts, shares his inmost thoughts and counsels (cp. *Od.* 13.303, 362, 376, 421; 17.360; 20.30). Even her transforming Odysseus into an old beggar is an extension of his own craftiness: he might well have disguised himself on his own initiative, as indeed he did on another occasion (cp. *Od.* 4.247). What we find is a communion of minds rather than help or collaboration. The instances of her presence are far more frequent and richer than the practical purpose of the story might require, as if Athena herself took delight in such a task.

Why is Athena so close to Odysseus? There is no mythical motive, no preexisting justification. Quite the contrary, Odysseus' violation of Athena's temple in Troy might have been expected to turn her against him.

The reason is internal to the action and the characters. We are given a clue in *Od.* 13.296ff.: Athena sees Odysseus as still wary, diffident, even suspicious of her after landing in Ithaca, and she asks him to relent, saying: "let us not argue . . . since you are of all mortals the best in wisdom and speech, whilst I among the gods am renowned for my mind and my guiles." Then again (13.330ff.): "Such is ever within you your thought: that is why in your sufferings I'll never leave you so well-spoken you are and sharp-witted and wise."

The dialogue simply confirms what the whole poem continually suggests. It is an affinity of spirit which produces the intimate solidarity between goddess and man. Any creative human quality, wonderful as it may be, suggests a divine power at its source, and there to bestow it or support it appears a god who, in turn, draws from this human contact a particular forcefulness. The intelligence of Odysseus is a divine spark; yet it gives Athena a distinctive physiognomy. It is as though the hero's spell conjured up the goddess, who refracts it, with intensified impact, upon the hero himself.

Much as Aphrodite is to Helen, Athena is to Odysseus: the divine and the human are twin aspects of the same reality. The impression of this rich complexity is again produced by the simplest means: dramatizing the moment and bringing the characters under its sway. Thus, in *Od.* 20.18ff., Odysseus, unable to sleep, addresses his heart on the eve of the final struggle, saying:

> Bear up, bear up, o my heart; / worse things you
>   suffered ere this,
> on the day when before me / by the dreadful Cyclops
>   devoured

were my goodly friends; / but you bore it, until mother
    wit
out of the cave led you forth / thinking that death was
    upon you.

And immediately after (20.30ff.):

                    . . . close to him came Athena
down from heaven descending; / like to a woman in
    shape.
over his head did she stand, / and thus she addressed
    him with words:
"Why do you lie still awake, / o most unhappy among
    men?
Here is the place of your home, / and your wife is here
    in it,
and your son—such is he / as none would not wish as
    his own."

Odysseus' *mētis*—his mind, intelligence, wit—is here hypos-
tatized as a self-standing power, as if it existed on its own
account, even apart from Odysseus himself. It is significant
that the very syntax of the passage is thrown off balance by
this discrepancy. The man's potentialities seem to take shape
and run beyond their boundaries. And here, in the intimacy
of Odysseus' solitude, Athena appears as a sustaining goddess. What does she do to help him? Nothing tangible. She
simply imparts a divine influence to Odysseus' moment of
self-realization.

The interventions of Athena thus do not detract from the
man. Rather, they intensify the focus that singles him out.
For the qualities so fostered by the goddess shine all the more
insofar as Odysseus is plunged into misery and woe. In suffering they find their ultimate proof. Here lies his true glory,

much more than in the fact that he finally succeeds in slaying his wife's suitors and regaining his kingdom. It was this view of Odysseus that must ultimately have prompted the legend of his further wanderings after returning to Ithaca (*Od.* 11.121ff.; 23.249ff., 268ff.).

As Homer saw him, Odysseus makes his grand entrance into the world. Free of moralistic distortions, he comes to us riding the waves, directly fed by the world's experience. To him belongs intellectual power nourished by the tensions of life. A subtler strain of character takes its place beside that of the warlike hero. Athena, at his side, is, in fieri, the future goddess of arts and crafts, the future goddess of wisdom. She shows his qualities sub specie aeternitatis. And yet even her presence is somehow transcended, surpassed. She is Odyssean as much as Odysseus is her votary. In this sense, it does not really make any difference whether she is materially present or not. Thus, when telling his story to the Phaeacians, Odysseus never mentions Athena; but her spirit, or the spirit she fosters, is nevertheless there. This is why the adventures so related have lent themselves to allegorization in many ways. Though we do not find the slightest trace of any symbolism, the very fact gives us pause: could we not read into the Cyclops brutal strength defeated by wit, into the Sirens the dangerous lure of the unknown, into Circe a sensuous spell, into the Lotus-eaters a fond dream of oblivion? But no, we conclude, there can be no allegory: each event is too real, too bright to be so interpreted. The reason is, rather, that these are no usual adventures. They combine action and thought. They challenge the understanding, the senses, and the imagination. Everywhere interfused is a lingering wonder, a thirst for knowledge, a spirit of wisdom. Even what is most raw is redeemed by a saving grace. They consist in neither mere narrative nor superimposed allegory, but, rather, the baffling meaning of any tension between opposing forces in the nature of things.

What, in this respect, is true of the action is also true of the character. But speculation, in Odysseus, is unaware of itself, spontaneously arising out of life's predicaments.

IX

A similar approach might apply to Penelope. Her very name became synonymous with "chaste," "faithful," or "virtuous" in the post-Homeric tradition—Horace or Ovid, for instance—just as Helen is considered wanton or Odysseus, crafty. In this spirit, any character could be developed in a one-sided, moralistic way.

Not so in Homer. It is remarkable that no such epithet as "chaste" or "faithful" is ever applied to Penelope there. Not even by calling her "wise," "prudent," or "careful" would we do her justice. Her broader, more comprehensive epithets (*periphrōn, ekhephrōn*) melt with her name: what we see is her earnest, pensive image, restrained by no compulsive morality but contained, rather, within its purity of form.

No more than Helen is wanton is Penelope prudish. Nor can we attribute to her any one particular mood. Sullen, melancholy, stern, indulgent—none of these applies either.

How, then, is Penelope a character? Again we find character in a fundamental sense: the person's image infused with life and characterized by the crucial stance in which it is perceived.

Penelope's first appearance in *Od.* 1.328ff. (see pp. 5–6 above) establishes the tone once and for all. The visual juxtaposition of the images is once again essential. She stands by the pillar of the hall, an object of vision and desire, the eyes of a hundred suitors gazing upon her. There is no need to explain, no need to dwell upon her power and her weakness, upon her silent attraction and her vulnerability. The picture itself is more enlightening than any comment could be. Repeated as it is elsewhere in the poem (16.414ff., 18.206ff., 21.63ff.), it is both timeless and immediate, typical and pertinent to the occasion. We seem to catch the supreme moment that makes it eternally significant: what the extremity of a woman's plight must always be.

But why does Penelope appear? Not, indeed, for the sake of her suitors, but to bid the minstrel to stop singing of the disastrous return of the Achaeans from Ilium:

> O Phemius, many there are / enchanting songs which you know—
> deeds of gods and of men / to which the minstrels give glory.
> Sing to them one of these, / sitting by; and let them in silence
> listen drinking their wine; / but, oh, refrain from this song—
> song of woe which upon me, / upon the heart deep within me,
> weighs evermore: most to me / has come this indelible pain.
> For so dear is that head / which I miss; the thought ever haunts me
> of the man whose renown / spreads wide through mid-Argos and Hellas.

How like Homer so to dramatize Penelope's state. We are reminded of Odysseus weeping at the song of Demodocus (*Od.* 8.83ff., 521ff.) or, though in a different way, of Helen and her web (see pp. 85–86 above)—all instances in which the characters are suddenly placed face-to-face with an image of their fate or of something that has deeply affected their lives. Phemius' song is, in its way, what Penelope's life is all about. Is her own grief to be a song for all to hear? She will not have it so; she would rather isolate herself in the intimacy of her thoughts, she would silence that encroaching voice. Her self-enclosed but intense nature is made evident.

But Telemachus rebukes her, and

> she, overcome with amazement, / made her way back to her room;
> what her son had so spoken, / pithy words, she laid in her heart;
> to the upper chamber she went / with the women that were her handmaids,
> and then wept for Odysseus, / her husband, till sleep
> sweet sleep fell on her eye-lids / shed by bright-eyed Athena.
> And the suitors made clamour / through the shades of the hall;
> all of them made a prayer / to sleep in love at her side.

Again a confrontation, now showing Penelope in a different light—resigned, submissive before Telemachus, who, having come of age, asserts his newly acquired strength. Is she amazed because of his unexpected energy and wisdom? Is she suddenly proud of him, not resenting his harshness? Her retreating figure gives us pause, concealing all complexities, while the attending clamor of the suitors heightens the moment of her exit: she leaves behind her the echo of a longing which is never fulfilled.

This opening scene presents Penelope for what she is throughout most of the *Odyssey*; it gives us a kernel, strikes a keynote that remains the same through its variations. But, one may object, if this is so, we only have a detached image;

and however splendid that may be, it has its limits: can it suffice, therefore, to convey a character such as Penelope is supposed to be? We might well imagine, by way of contrast, how a novelist would have traced through the years a woman so plagued by suitors during the long absence of her husband; at the end the story would yield the full-fledged character, who had moved from a modest beginning through some central climax.

But in Homer, as always, the first appearance is complete in itself. We have a few crucial moments, each of them a center in its own right, and yet all conspiring to summon up the complex image of a hero—Hector, for instance, in his advances and retreats—the sense of time made palpable in the movement itself.

How can such a treatment be applied to Penelope? The task was more difficult, for her drama is an inward one. It is a story of patience, resistance, hope, fear, expectation—all emotions buried deep within her. And she remains fixed in one unchanging condition and place where nothing intrudes except the suitors, whose comings and goings become a daily routine. How to convey the day-to-day struggle, the long years, life and love waning, yet an inner resilience that keeps Penelope's integrity alive?

The recurring scenes—whether repeated literally or not—play an important part here. While they are narratively pertinent, they also convey a way of being, a persisting cadence in the course of existence. Take again, in the passage just commented upon, the recurring appearance of Penelope by the pillar of the hall. It has the effect of a statue or a painting and, as such, transcends the moment that produces it. This woman appearing in her splendor yet veiled, proud and modest at the same time, delivers her message even before she does or says anything. If the passage were a fragment and the rest of the poem were lost, we might still divine its context. Set astir by the immediacy of the image, we would recompose for it a perspective of time and place. As it is, Homer completes the picture for us, realizing what is implied; but the scene itself is prophetic of what is to come, attuning us to modes of being rather than gradual characterizations.

Or take, in the same passage, Telemachus' rebuke. It occurs again later (in 21.350ff., cp. 17.45ff.) and is an example of his occasional self-righteousness toward his mother (18.228ff., 20.131ff.). Penelope, on the other hand, is resigned, submissive to her son. Here again is an image as constant as it is evoked by the occasion—that of a mother withdrawing to her room, yielding to the high-handed young son who has just become a man. It is not that Penelope is weak; nor is it a question of passing moods. We see, rather, an inevitable condition, the universal circumstance of parents outgrown by their offspring. The sense of passing time and of growth is thus instantly worked into Penelope's image, without any need to dwell upon her years. Her vital womanhood is tinged with submissive mellowness. The outcry of the suitors and the sharpness of Telemachus bring out these opposing qualities in her.

In the same passage, we see Penelope going up to her chamber and crying for Odysseus until sleep comes upon her. Again, a recurring outline intrinsic to our idea of Penelope (*Od.* 4.787, 793f.; 16.449ff.; 18.187ff., 302; 19.600ff.; 21.356ff.). Here the recurrence is more frequent, more constant, and the sense of time more intense, the theme of her grief merging incessantly with the continuous succession of night and day. She never remains for long in the great hall. Either a behest of Telemachus or her own inner need drives her back to her room as to a vantage-ground. Here her tears are free to flow; and here, every time, sweet sleep is shed upon her by the goddess Athena. From solitude and inwardness comes the strength in sadness. She is passionate, not resigned. But what makes Penelope memorable and so impresses her upon the imagination is the persistency of these recurring scenes. It is as though the rhythm of natural time were intensified by this interplay of waking and sleeping, by so rendering the exhaustion of weeping on the one hand and the blessing of recovery on the other.

Dreams and omens, too, play their part: her far-distant sister Iphthime reassures her about Telemachus' safety (*Od.* 4.795ff.) and Odysseus himself portends his return (19.545ff., 20.87). Produced as they are by the long anguish of a constantly recurring thought and yet pointing to a brighter future, such dreams crystallize into present form the indefinite range of memories, hopes, and fears. What has long been brewing is instantly dramatized. Penelope's state finds its transparent symbolism; it is objectified, opened up to the reader's imagination rather than presented in terms that require an interpreter of dreams. A similarly dramatic effect is achieved by Phemius' song.

And last but not least, the thrice-told tale of the web (*Od.* 2.93ff., 19.138ff., 24.128ff.). It is, of course, meant to be a stratagem, but, as such, it is, we must admit, rather weak. Why, then, is it so suggestive, so famous? Because that weaving and unweaving seems to give palpable form to the long succession of days and nights lived alone by Penelope. Here is patience and resistance far more than wiliness. Just as the pain of her waking thoughts is lulled by sleep, so she unweaves by night what she weaves by day. What other evidence is there of her wiliness? We twice find (*Od.* 2.91f., 13.380f.): "to all does she give some hope—a promise, a message; but other longings are in her mind." What promises, what messages? Homer does not tell us; he deals with the complexities of life, not those of intrigue. And Penelope thus weaves her threads of life—thoughts ever turning upon themselves day in day out. The guile consists in knowing how to do it for so long without being destroyed.

Another element that enables Homer to transcend the limitations of the circumscribed image is the sense of place. For a place, whether a room or a piece of land, has a solid permanence of its own. It continuously exists in its own right and yet, by being constantly associated with our daily acts, becomes an integral part of our lives. By the same token, separate moments find in place an accustomed focus, draw from it a strong consistency; and what otherwise would only be a casual appearance or a person's elusive image appears anchored at a vantage point. Such is eminently the case with Penelope. "I shall go up to my chamber; I shall lie upon my bed, that place filled with my sighs, ever stained with my tears, since the day when Odysseus sailed off to Ilium," she says more than once (*Od.* 17.102ff., 19.595ff.). Like the famous loom, her chamber or bed is charged with experience and life and becomes symbolic of revolving time. There she always returns after leaving the hall. We could hardly imagine her elsewhere. Her grief seems as enduring as the walls that enclose her.

Or the house itself. Thinking of the day when she might have to depart with one of her suitors, Penelope says over and over again (*Od.* 19.579ff., 21.77ff.), ". . . and ah, leave behind me this house of my love, this beautiful house so filled with the substance of life; the thought of it will ever be with me, even in dreams." It is the "great, high-roofed, well-built house" which wandering Odysseus sees in his mind's eye (*Od.* 7.225, cp. 6.315, 10.474, etc.). Penelope, though living in it, imagines it for a moment as a faraway dream. It thus becomes, for her also, the object of infinite longing, as if it embodied a way of life, a happiness that might have been, or that perhaps might still be——.

Or take the pillar by which Penelope stands when appearing before the suitors, a solid shape that seems to share and affirm her impassive attitude toward them, recording it in stone. And we might add the chair upon which she sits before the fire when talking intimately with Odysseus disguised as a beggar (*Od.* 19.55ff., cp. 17.97), a spot which, by the very fact of being different, seems to acquire distinctive value, as if it were reserved for rarer moments of familiar intercourse and thus gives them a permanent setting.

Homer, as we have seen, never *describes* a house or a landscape. He hardly ever mentions an object except insofar as it is seen, touched, experienced, or in any way brought into contact with a particular act. Now this general feature of Homeric style has an essential bearing on Penelope as a character. Through recurrent association, things become part and parcel of her being. They blend with her daily acts and inmost thoughts, giving them locality and focus. She grows upon us enriched by her environment. We do not see her as someone who must, as usual, necessarily live in a certain place. Rather, she *is* the place. It is her raison d'être, her strength. The idea of leaving it is like death. The fact of staying is at one with the integrity of her life, as if her habitation were nature itself, infusing her with a vital juice even in her grief.

Here is a human quality that defies direct expression. By so relying on the silent eloquence of things, Homer lets it transpire through Penelope's image. For when she speaks, she seldom says anything new. Her utterances often resemble a refrain: "My beauty the gods destroyed, ever since he sailed off in his ships" (*Od.* 18.180, cp. 251, 19.124); "for Odysseus ever yearning, my heart is melting away" (19.136, 18.204,

1.343); "if he came to keep watch on my life, greater would be my renown" (18.254, 19.127). This is inevitable. If Penelope gave us more details about herself, the purity of the image would be impaired. We would miss her poise, her way of life, the bond that naturally and yet mysteriously keeps her in unison with her world.

Like other Homeric characters, Penelope eludes definition because her makeup is so concrete, so fused with a place or a pose. Perhaps we get nearest to an interpretation of her character in the words addressed to Odysseus by his mother's shade (*Od.* 11.181ff., cp. 16.37, 13.337): "Verily she does remain with steadfast heart in the house: the languishing nights and the days ever wane upon her in tears." "Steadfast heart"—the Greek *tetlēoti thymō* tells it better. Homer's *tetlēoti* conveys resistance, patience, suffering. The quality is not expressed as a moral attribute but as a state of being. For Penelope it means standing her ground, remaining in her place. The same phrase is used for Odysseus in the Cyclops' cave (*Od.* 9.435); but it occurs most frequently in reference to Penelope. The epic of heroic exploits is here silenced; but no less heroism is instilled into the quiet image of Penelope.

In the final part of the *Odyssey* Penelope's inner ferment comes more clearly into the open. The entrance of disguised Odysseus into the great hall injects a new dramatic element. His ill-treatment at the hands of the suitors and the uproar which ensues attract her attention. She hears from her room, she sees and sympathizes with the mysterious stranger. This vivid, spontaneous interest seems to take her out of herself. She becomes freer, more articulate. The first climax comes when she suddenly wishes to appear in the hall before the suitors (*Od.* 18.158ff.):

> And her mind was now prompted / by the goddess
>   bright-eyed Athena
>
> . . . .
>
> to stand in front of her suitors / and so fan up in full
>   measure
> the heart's desire within them, / while lovelier she
>   might appear
> in the eyes of husband and son, / lovelier than ever
>   before.
> A helpless laughter came from her, / she spoke out and
>   she called:
> "Eurynome, a wish is in me, / such as I never had,
> of showing myself to the suitors / however hateful they
>   are. . . ."

What does this divine influence purport? Why does Penelope laugh? The Greek is hard to translate. Fitzgerald has: "knowing no reason, laughing confusedly," John Finley offers: "aimless laughter," Chapman interprets further: "to shew her humor bore no serious appetite to that light show." This laughter is unexplained but not groundless or frivolous, as Chapman implies. Penelope is laughing at herself, at this new sensation of hers. It is as if the newcomer had caused a momentary shift in her thoughts, and she could now look at life objectively, even at the suitors, who are, in spite of everything, men. Perhaps the irony of existence dawns on her. Be that as it may, what stands out is the laughing image itself—how solidly self-enclosed it is and yet full of suggestion. If Penelope were *explained*, we should merely have an additional trait. As it is, we have infinite implications.

This existential laughter comes, not insignificantly, in a moment of beauty and expanded emotions. While Penelope is readying herself to face the suitors, a beautifying sleep is

cast upon her through the magic of Athena. She soon wakes
(199):

> Then, wiping, she rubbed her face / with both her
>   hands and she said:
> "Really upon my dread woes / a soft strange sleep cast
>   its shroud.
> I would that a death so soft / came upon me from
>   Artemis holy
> right now. . . .

She wipes her face, is if to clear away all drowsiness—a significant gesture in Homer, who is so chary of casual detail.
Then she prays. Again we are given pause. How do we explain her wish for death at this point? Why does it come now
and not before? Why does it coincide with this restoring sleep
and greater fullness of being? The reason is that Penelope has
reached a peak of experience. Things are clearer. She can now
realize her condition rather than merely suffer it. No more
resignation, no more compromise. Beauty and life are not to
be tampered with. Only by dying can one save them from
cheap encroachment. And grief, released from habit, turns
into infinite longings that can only find their fulfillment in the
thought of death. Later on (*Od.* 20.61ff.), Penelope enriches
such a thought with the poetry of myth. There is strength,
there is imagination in her sadness.

The plot is here the screen of a refined psychology that
cannot be explained in terms of factual details external to the
moment; for these (e.g., Odysseus' behest that Penelope re-
marry if he should not return, Telemachus' coming of age and
his impatience) are as true now as they were before. No, what
is vital in Penelope's state of mind comes from the scene itself,
the immediate action. Homer, as always, brings into full play
the juxtaposition of images, the effect of the characters on one

another as they stand in dramatic contiguity. Penelope has witnessed the striking of Odysseus. Her spirits are roused. She is summoned to new life. Now she can defiantly be herself, she can face the suitors on her own initiative, can rebuke Telemachus for being weak rather than being rebuffed by him. What is more, the sudden flush of emotion permeates her being. She is transfigured, enhanced both in energy and looks. Athena's beautifying spell comes within this purview. As elsewhere (see above, p. 33), the goddess only reinforces a quality that is already there (cp. *Od.* 17.37). Or, rather, the divine element is intrinsic to what is happening on the human level. It is one with the quickened movement of the action, one with the mysterious animation of the whole scene. And it is reflected in Penelope. Her beauty becomes a sense of power, as if her life were now in her own hands, to live out— or to let go.

Here is yet another example of Homer's concreteness. Each thing stands out in its full dimension: hence the simplicity of the means and also the unfathomable implications. What comes to the fore is, quite simply, the reciprocity of the positions of the characters in their setting as they sit or stand or move in one another's sight, projecting their images. A presence, an arrival, or a departure is paramount. Thus the entrance of disguised Odysseus into the hall starts off a new phase, just as, in the composition of a painting, even a slight point of relief imparts a new perspective. Penelope is immediately drawn into the magic circuit, her immediate interest in the stranger almost unaware of itself.

The hall remains the same, like a stage set that does not change from act to act. Penelope's appearance echoes the one at the beginning of the poem. The persistence of the imagery sharpens our sense of her altered state rather than weakening it. Thus our indifferent walls, ever the same, ring with another voice than yesterday's, and the change becomes solemn through contrast. What strikes us is existence, or the condition of life, rather than an episode brought about by the plot.

The interplay of images becomes more penetrating and revealing in the conversation between Penelope and the still disguised Odysseus, at night, by the fire of the hall (*Od.* 19.103ff.). Quite cast aside is the requirement of the plot that Odysseus should test Penelope (19.45, cp. 16.304ff.); forgotten or underplayed is the element of disguise as a mere device to achieve victory. What prevails is mutual magnetism, sympathy, warmth, progressive intimacy.

How is this effect achieved? It would be difficult to single out any particular passage. What Penelope says as she dwells upon her desperate state or upon human life is simple enough; and Odysseus' tale may stir her but not win her over. What stands out more than anything else is the situation itself, the moment and place, the face-to-face relation. The images of both characters are imbued with silent force, as if the fate of one were about to meet with that of the other; and the contiguity itself produces a communion that lies beyond expression in words.

Thus, quite unsolicited, Penelope starts to disclose to the old beggar the drama of her life (129ff.); it is, at times, as if she were just thinking aloud or finding relief in speech (510ff.):

> We'll go to bed soon enough, / the time of soft rest is approaching
> for those whom sleep enfolds, / sweet sleep, whatever their cares.
> But not for me; boundless pain / was given to me by the gods.

> As the day passes on, / I weep and wail, but find
>   pleasure
> seeing to my tasks and to those / of the handmaids
>   busy in the house;
> But at the fall of night, / when sleep enfolds all the
>   rest,
> I lie down on my bed, / and my inmost heart is
>   encompassed
> with sharp cares that come thronging / and kindle the
>   throes of my grief.

Here, in a way unusual for Homer, she sums up experience; elsewhere she dwells on her most pressing and secret concerns: on whether or not to accept one of the suitors, or on Telemachus, who wants to be his own master and would have her leave. Always, whatever she says, there is the same urgency in her to hear, to speak. With whom else can Penelope share her thoughts?—not with the homely Eurycleia or Eurynome, not with the patronizing Telemachus. But here is a mysterious stranger who has traveled far and wide, a worldly-wise old man with persuasive and insinuating ways; and her pent-up human warmth finds a way to come into the open: she becomes responsive, expansive, free, unconventional. Yes, here at last is a friend. "No one dearer than you ever came to this house," she says to him (351), and (589f.): "If only you would, O stranger, ever sit in the hall at my side and give me delight; sleep would not come on my eyelids."

Considered in this light, even the disguise and the lies of Odysseus might be seen as a way to the truth. For twenty years have passed; everything has suffered change; a long, blank interval has to be filled; and things must now be exhumed or summoned back to life delicately, tentatively, gradually. Odysseus' half-truths help restore the broken continuity without any abrupt revelation which, in this case, would have required a pathetic scene quite alien to Homer's concreteness. When the beggar in disguise tells Penelope of Odysseus' clothes or of his stay in Crete and "mixes truth with falsehood," he achieves that subtle effect which is wrought upon us by things vividly remembered but displaced. A further effort might retrieve the lost context. If the thing so remembered is dear to the heart and is brought home by a sympathetic messenger, intuition conspires with love to restore the past and translate it into present feeling, even if the missing links cannot be divined. Penelope is halfway to such realization, even though she does not know it. Hence her tears of tenderness, beautifully brought out by the simile of melting snow (205ff.; see pp. 165–66).

The path to recognition and reunion is hard—not only factually, but mentally. It implies in Penelope, and also in Odysseus, a complex mental process. We must do it justice and not look at it in terms of preordained plan. Even the guile or transformation of Odysseus will then have an aesthetic function—to bring out elusive strains in Penelope's character. This was indeed the natural way in Homer's art. Instead of a passionate soliloquy or a description of inner states, we have a response to alleged facts and objects filled with intimate significance. The very shape and condition of the wandering beggar suggest Odysseus; his tale and lies suggest him in an even more pointed and poignant way; the mention of a cloak or brooch he wore summons up a flood of passionate memories. How often we are touched by resemblances, associations! The impact of these ambiguities comes suddenly, unawares, with a forceful subtlety denied to direct experience—as if the nature of things conspired with emotion. Penelope thus enters her new state fitfully, indirectly. She is all at once tender, perceptive, and nervously alive—like one who, without knowing it, is on the verge of some unsuspected happiness.

The same might be said about the famous dream she finally tells Odysseus (535–52). Its purport from the viewpoint of the plot is obvious enough. But the contents is richer than that. If, in the dream, she delights in the sight of her geese suddenly killed by an eagle claiming to be Odysseus, who will likewise kill the suitors, why her delight in the geese that symbolize the suitors? And why, after the dream, does she anxiously look out to reassure herself that the geese are still right there where they always were, feeding as before? There is no need to press the symbolism. Here again the imagery is suggestive of character. Those geese give us a glimpse into Penelope's daily life: how sudden and bright and clear do they appear again in their daylight reality after the tempestuous dream; how satisfying their presence, even in the dream, before the eagle arrives! Here is the earthy joy of domesticity at its simplest level. It inevitably blends with the existence of the suitors, but it is nevertheless strongly rooted in its own right; and it is reflected in those indifferent geese that are so removed from the personal problems of any character. In this respect, the eagle of the dream certainly implies upheaval, change, violence. It is as though there were trepidation in Penelope before the approaching storm, before she decides to set for her suitors the contest of the bow.

The silent interplay of images is more significant than ever in the final scene of recognition and reunion (*Od.* 23.1–296). Penelope, asleep in her room, has been spared the horror of the killing; then, awakened and told the tidings, she comes down, incredulous, to the hall. Let us join her at this point (85ff.):

> . . . and intensely her heart
> was wavering whether aloof / she should speak and
>   question her husband
> or going forth right up close / should kiss his face, clasp
>   his hands.
> But after coming within / and crossing the threshold of
>   stone,
> she sat in front of Odysseus, / face-to-face, in the light
>   of the fire,
> at the side of the opposite wall; / while he, against the
>   tall pillar,
> sat looking down on the floor, / expecting to hear the
>   voice
> of his lovely wife any moment, / whenever her eyes
>   had beheld him.
> For long in silence she sat, / and amazement entered
>   her heart:
> as she looked, at one time / she would fix her gaze on
>   his face,
> at another, she would not know . . .

". . . face-to-face, in the light of the fire, at the side of the opposite wall"; "he, against the tall pillar . . ."—what elsewhere would be a descriptive detail here becomes an integrating element of the figure placed before us, not so much to set it off, as to give it its indispensable breathing space, position, and perspective. The physical contours thus merge with the moment of approach and realization. Hence Penelope's breathtaking presence—her silence, her wonder, her gaze. She startles us in her stillness, her simple poise solemnized by the surrounding space. We watch, we wait, like Odysseus; and yet we take delight in the richness of the implications: an untold inner tumult is resolved into form.

Should she fly into her husband's arms? speak first? These insufficient alternatives are cast aside the moment Penelope enters the hall. Just awakened from her deep sleep (compare her sleep in 18.187ff.), she is newborn into a different world. Her long dream has come true; and yet it must be intimately realized; she must take her bearings and step softly into her future. It is not so much a question of recognizing Odysseus as of knowing herself and bringing things into tune with experience. But Telemachus, in his youthful self-sufficiency, does not understand. "O mother, no mother," he says, "O hard of heart, why do you so stand away from my father. . . ?" Odysseus smiles. "Let her alone"; he says, "she will soon know me better"; and he attends to other business. Penelope remains withdrawn, observant, and introspective.

Later Athena beautifies Odysseus; and, appearing in all his pristine splendor to Penelope who is still sitting in silence, "O inscrutable woman," he cries out, "you are surely void of all feeling!," as if he himself were now wooing her. His transformation into a beautiful man hardly impresses her: what matters is her inner tension, not the effect of any outward sign. She says at last, unprotesting, "I am not proud, not indifferent, not dumb-struck; well I know how you looked when you set sail"; and then, turning to Eurycleia with the unfailing sagacity of instinct, "But come now, O Eurycleia, lay out for him the soft bed outside the well-built chamber which he once made himself." At this point she strikes home; Odysseus is enraged: how could she make so light of their secret—the bedstead fashioned by his own hands, the room built over it? And with passionate precision he proceeds to tell how he worked these things piece by piece. Now Penelope can no longer resist; in tears, she rushes to embrace and kiss him.

Is, then, Penelope convinced only by the proof of the

bed? No. Let us not take the passage too literally. Especially here do we find that significance which Homer confers on material objects through their human associations. The bed of Penelope and Odysseus is symbolic of itself; it summons up their whole youth; its secrecy conveys the sense of intimacies both past and yet to come, bridging the gap of years. Homer draws the utmost meaning from the material at his disposal: the bed thus ceases to be the raw traditional device of recognition often found in ancient tales; what matters is its force of suggestion. When Odysseus recounts so fervently how he built it, he is really telling the story of his love. No wonder Penelope is overwhelmed. As she listens, she pictures again the young Odysseus hard at work, the years of separation roll away. "The gods begrudged it us to enjoy our youth at each other's side," she says; but their secret bed is there to receive them once again, and what was lost can be retrieved all at once. She continues to speak. Like her previous wonder, like the bed itself, her simple words imply much more than it might seem at first. "O Odysseus, do not be angry, you who are the wisest of men . . . do not resent it if earlier I showed not my love as I do now." Yes, wisdom is needed, and intelligence, to understand the human complexities of the moment—a sympathetic insight is required from Odysseus as well as from the reader. "My spirit was in a shudder lest any man might beguile me": here is mistrust not merely of Odysseus but of her own susceptibilities, and a delight so sudden as to be unsure of itself. "Helen would not have lain in the bed of love with a stranger, had she known . . .": how significant of Penelope to compare herself with Helen and not Clytaemnestra, and to do so in sympathy, as if she herself were not immune from temptation. "But now you have made the signs clear—the signs of that bed that none ever saw but we alone": secrecy so stressed transcends the importance of the bed as a mere object of recognition; it is a way of referring to what is so intimate in experience as to defy direct expression.

At last comes the long embrace (233ff.):

> As when welcome the earth / appears to men that are
>   swimming
> struck by the god Poseidon, / their well-wrought ship
>   out at sea
> shattered while driven hard / by the swelling waves
>   and the wind;
> only a few of them escape / from the foaming sea to the
>   land
> swimming, and very dense / the brine makes a crust on
>   their skin,
> with joyous welcome they step / upon land, escaped
>   from their doom;
> so dear, so welcome her husband / was there in the
>   sight of her eyes,
> and from his neck not at all / she let go loose her white
>   arms.

We are reminded of the simile depicting Odysseus when he sights the coast of Scheria (*Od.* 5.394ff.):

> As when most dear, most desired / appears to children
>   the life
> of a father lying down in sickness, / afflicted with
>   terrible pains
> slowly wasting away, / a malignant fate is upon him,
> and to dear joy he is at last / released by the gods from
>   his doom;
> so dear, so welcome to Odysseus / appeared the earth
>   and the forest.

What indeed could be dearer? Life and the bounties of earth
suddenly restored against all hope to a shipwrecked swimmer, health restored to a dying man—this is a primordial joy
which is, at the same time, prophetic of all other joys. Such
is the return of Odysseus to Penelope. Her love finds here its
fullest expression. Homer could hardly state the tenderness
of its complexities, its infinite longings; but in the simile
everything is implied: love, though unmentioned, is the driving force, and it comes all at once, floodlike, as vital as breath,
as bounteous as life.

Penelope is central to this scene. The simile refers more
particularly to her. It is her we see embracing, not Odysseus—
a prolonged embrace which, again, stills into form a turmoil
of unspoken emotions. She entirely overshadows Odysseus,
who, on his part, at last finds himself feeling a moment of
tenderness. Indeed, Penelope grows on us and becomes the
dominant character from book 18 onward. We never see her
again after this scene, and the rest of the poem is an anti-
climax. It is as if Homer wished, here, to give her her due, to
picture in her person the dignity of life itself, quite apart from
the glamor of resounding deeds. As implied in the similes
just quoted, her inner storms were no less severe than those
undergone by Odysseus, but were unseen, unrecorded, only
shadowed forth in such forms as the tale of the web or her
vigils, dreams, prayers. A mysterious ferment transpires from
her quiet image; and she baffles our imagination more than
Odysseus can.

X

We know little of Penelope's background. She is simply
what she is on the strength of any single passage that brings
her to the fore. Mythical context and moralistic preconceptions are swept aside by the way Homer focuses on the con-

crete moment as it comes to life. By singling out a thing, he
saves it from the encroachment of external connections and
vindicates it in the truth of its own nature.

Homer's concreteness thus has the widest implications.
Even minor characters hold their own, have a dominating
position wherever or whenever they appear. It is as if they
existed in themselves and by themselves. Rather than their
furthering the plot, the reverse might be true: the plot is so
conceived as to bring them into the limelight.

This is the case with Nausicaa. From the viewpoint of
the plot, she is, of course, no more than a means to an end.
Athena arranges for her to go do the washing by the seashore
so that Odysseus may meet her and, once introduced to the
king, her father, prevail upon the Phaeacians to take him back
to Ithaca.

But nothing is more alien to Homer than to emphasize
the mechanism of the plot. What we find is simple juxtaposition or coincidence of time and place. Odysseus' arrival coincides with Nausicaa's coming of age; and she has a dream.
Though it is Athena's work, what more natural than that the
dream should be of love and marriage, bringing to mind suitors and clothes that need washing so that, brightly clad, she
may all the more be admired?

Filled with wonder, Nausicaa awakes and runs to her
father. "Let me have the chariot and mules," she says in short,
"your clothes need washing and so do those of my brothers."
The poet adds (*Od.* 6.66):

> So she said; she felt shame / to mention the flourishing
> wedding
> to her dear father, but he / understood all her thoughts
> and so spoke. . . .

We see her later near the river-mouth. After the washing she plays and dances with her companions (*Od.* 6.101ff.):

> And with them then Nausicaa / white-armed gave start to the dance.
> Even as Artemis strides, / on the mountains, goddess-of-arrows,
> either upon Erymanthus / or upon lofty Taygetus,
> taking delight in the boars / or in the swift-footed deer,
> and along with her the nymphs / daughters-of-Zeus-aegis-bearing
> over the wilderness sport. / And Leto rejoices at heart;
> for higher up than all others / she holds her head and her brow,
> and clearly does she stand out, / although all of them are lovely;
> such among her companions / stood out the maiden unwedded.

The timid girl of a few moments before now appears in all her beauty. The dream suddenly awoke in her a new spirit of initiative in asking for the chariot, followed by shame, the innocent lie, the flush that gave her away. Here by the sea those fleeting states of mind are forgotten. The simile, with its picture of Artemis and her nymphs ranging over the mountains, conveys a sense of freedom, movement, wild places. It does much more than present Nausicaa as more beautiful than her companions. She flashes out in the glow of youth. The glory of the moment is upon her. She exerts her spell, unaware of her own powers.

When Odysseus, naked, comes out of his hiding place, all the other girls run away at the horrendous sight. She alone remains (*Od.* 6.139ff.):

Alcinous' daughter alone / remained, for in her Athena
touched with courage her heart, / removed all fear from
    her limbs;
before him she stood in suspense. . . .

Here is a further step; the development is pursued in strong
visual outline: she is no longer exulting in movement, but is
a still figure, self-reliant, poised in her own strength. Whence
this quiet courage? Athena's touch is one and all with her
new-blown feelings; and her stillness shows her now thoughtful, earnest, expectant.

Odysseus' glorious praises do not ruffle her; but they sink
deep. Later when, after washing himself, he appears again,
beautified by Athena, she says to her companions (*Od.*
6.244ff.):

Would he were mine / such a man, my husband in very
    name
right here having his dwelling; / ah, that it pleased him
    to stay.

These words, which have scandalized some commentators,
are really characteristic of Nausicaa. The train of feeling and
thought initiated by the dream cannot but run its full course.
That spirit of youth cannot be conventional, cannot be restrained by propriety. Her imagination is free.

Similar remarks can be made about Telemachus. He is
the central character in the first four books of the *Odyssey,* so
much so that scholars have spoken of the *Telemachy* as a separate poem. But, again, here is a fine example of the way in
which Homer juxtaposes things rather than subordinating
them to one another. He gives a strong separate existence to
any character claiming a vital moment.

What stands out, as in the case of Nausicaa, is Telemachus' time of life. How typical it is of Homer not to introduce him or explain him, but immediately to present him simply as a youth in distress and bearing the burden of his ripening age. For straightaway we see him sitting in the midst of his mother's suitors, grieving and day-dreaming about his father (*Od.* 1.113). Such is the state of early youth at odds with the world—sensitive, passionate, and yet passive, lost in dreams, incapable of action.

But here is also a latent strength; the fullness of maturity will soon bring it out. Telemachus' vision of his father contains the seed of imminent development: it is hope that he will return; it is silent insurrection against the usurpers; and it is thus also a sense of power within himself, a striving toward manhood. His state is, unwittingly, a moment of expectation, as if the future were casting its shadow on the present. And then, as a visitor, Athena comes in the shape of old Mentes; talking to the young man, questioning him, encouraging him, reminding him of his father, she stirs him from his dream. What she says to him later (*Od.* 2.270ff.) is relevant here:

> Not now nor tomorrow, O Telemachus, / will you be a
>   fool or a weakling,
> if it is true that in you / your father's high might is
>   instilled,
> such as he was in realizing / the force of deeds and of
>   words. . . .

Is it not as if Athena were here a goddess of growth, a *kourotrophos*? Her touch brings to swift fruition the potentialities of the youth.

The effect is indeed sudden. What makes it powerful is, again, the enactment of the scene itself: the earnest face-to-

face presence, the growing intimacy of the dialogue, divine
impact and human receptivity. At the end Athena vanishes
like a bird. Wonder fills Telemachus; he becomes aware that
a god was speaking to him.

And now he is possessed of renewed powers. He confronts his mother's suitors; and his voice is fuller, his words
resolute; those who hear him are amazed. Restlessly active,
he must go on the quest for his father. It is Athena, of course,
who tells him to do so; but, again, is not this spirit of initiative
all one with his incipient manhood? All the more since his
quest serves no practical purpose: Odysseus will return an-
yway. "I sent him, so that he might win glory for himself,"
Athena explains later in the poem. But what glory? No more
than the glory of really being what he is—to be seen, heard,
known. And we see Telemachus going out into the world at
Pylos and Sparta, shy at first, but gradually more and more
master of himself.

Thus, when visiting Nestor, he asks Athena, who accom-
panies him in the shape of Mentor (*Od.* 3.21):

> Mentor, how shall I approach, / how shall I greet him,
>   how speak?
> Not yet am I master of words / nor of wisdom in
>   speech.
> Shame does a young man feel / in addressing one that
>   is old.

And Athena replies:

> Telemachus, some words yourself / in your own heart
>   you'll think out,
> and others will one of the gods / suggest to you. I do
>   not think

that without the will of the gods / you came to light
  and grew up.

In such delicate moments of approach a young man first
comes into his own. He wonders at the world while realizing
who he is; his natural restraint is matched by a no less natural
desire to overcome it. And a mysterious power appears to be
at work. A god, says Athena; and yet that god is no other
than herself. But what is she on this occasion? A divine touch
that taps the potentialities of nature and, at the same time, a
most intimate prompting of personal capacities.

Nausicaa and Telemachus are parallel characters. Different as they are from each other, the same stress of time or
the same ripeness of the moment brings them to the fore. For,
in both cases, Homer has precipitated into one occasion that
process of life which we might rather convey in the shape of
a biography; and he has done so by simply bringing the youth
and the maiden into a pregnant point of contact with the
action. Odysseus' approach touches both their lives to the
quick. They suddenly come out of their niches. While they
do, everything else falls into the background. Even Athena
and Odysseus recede: they are but witnesses of their presence
and growth.

What is so poignantly true of Nausicaa and Telemachus
is also true—though more generally, less strikingly—of all the
other characters summoned into existence by Odysseus' approach or arrival. How, for instance, do we come to know the
swineherd Eumaeus and why is he so memorable? It is because he is so firmly established where he is, his daily tasks
rendered in a few phrases that typify his existence, as if he
were one with the place itself; and yet, when approached by
the disguised Odysseus, he is stirred to quickening sympathy,

allured into a mood of communication and confession, and thus made ready to play his part. We recognize the same kind of rapid characterization in the herdsman Philoitius (*Od.* 20.185ff.) and, on the other hand, the goatherd Melanthius (17.212ff.). And how do we come to know the suitors? Why are they so vivid in our imagination, quite apart from the story? Again, because right from the beginning we find them strongly fixed where they are through recurring scenes of banqueting and reveling, entrenched in a position that grows dramatically precarious as Odysseus draws near.

There is no need for the poet to go out of his way to judge or qualify a character. Eumaeus or Philoitius is no more praised than Melanthius is blamed. What we see and remember is the evidence of each scene. Each and all inevitably take position on the eve of Odysseus' return or in his immediate presence. Character, with the attending emotions, is produced by the crisis itself.

In the same way, such mythical figures as Calypso and Circe are suddenly drawn out of their eternal dream to taste the bittersweet fruits of human life; and we can only catch the song of the Sirens for a moment, as Odysseus' ship passes by. Even the eternal peace of the gods is all at once interrupted and disturbed by concern for Odysseus's return; only in relation to his movements does Athena find occasion to manifest her power. It is difficult to imagine what these divine beings would do, were he not there. It is as if Odysseus gave them a piercing, momentary summons. Then and there they stand out in solitary relief.

XI

The same kind of genius that singled out Nausicaa and Telemachus over and above the requirements of the plot is more or less at work everywhere. The poems can be seen as arrays of images which any particular moment of the action might independently bring to the fore. The first inkling is a visual one. A mere body, standing on its own strength or poised for action, cannot but suggest a life of its own. This individualizing touch is essential to the delineation of any vital character.

Such effect is richly shown in the battle scenes of the *Iliad*. It has often been said that Homer presents us with man-to-man fighting or simple heroes, and that he usually ignores the multitude. It would be false to ascribe this singling out of heroes to a desire to exclude commoners from a world of princes or to the legends of which the heroes are protagonists. The real reason, intrinsic to Homer's art, is delight in the perception of any full-bodied figure instantly exerting vital strength.

For instance, take *Il*. 13.156ff.:

> Deiphobos there in their midst / was striding forth in
>   high spirits
> and before him he held / the shield even-spaced-on-all-
>   sides,
> with nimble steps stepping out, / shield-covered
>   extending his footsteps;
> and Meriones upon him / aimed the bright-pointed
>   spear. . . .

This is a typical passage. The general battle is merely hinted at; the field of vision converges to a point of focus—one spot, one moment, in which a figure strongly stands out to meet the impending destiny. It is as though we were looking at a large fresco: there is the general effect, but our attention immediately goes to a certain figure, movement, pose, or gesture.

The figures that thus emerge often strike us for a moment, and they are gone. How and when do they become real characters? That depends on how far they realize their identity in the expanding occasion which brings them to the fore. The warrior's figure then becomes an image that stays in our minds; and as the image grows in consistency, it coruscates, draws attention from all sides, creates space around itself. For the same reason, it comes to suggest duration, it appears to embody experience. Such, for instance, is the case with Asios in *Il.* 12.110ff., or Euphorbos in 17.9ff.

Such fleeting characterizations are not confined to battle scenes. This image-making power is not a technique adapted to a particular subject matter. It is a matter of perception and expression. It can be brought to bear upon any object that strikes the imagination.

A case in point is Thersites (*Il.* 2.211ff.). Why has he achieved immortal fame, though he appears in only one passage of the *Iliad*? Is it because he appears to be a commoner? Or because of his unusual role and features?

No, these are curiosities, details. The reason lies, again, in the concrete, life-giving touch. Thersites is suddenly set off in high relief, isolated from the multitude of men who have just been roused to sail for home and are being checked by Odysseus.

"Thersites alone, unbridled of tongue, was still brawling," says the poet; and there we see him—an awkward, grotesque figure—attacking Agamemnon under the gaze of the approving bystanders:

> O Atreides, what is it / you still complain of and need?
> filled with bronze are your tents / and many women
>   therein

are kept enclosed: / the choicest that we, the people, to
    you—

to you first of all ever offer, / whenever we capture a
    town.

Is it now gold as well / that you want—the gold that
    from Troy

some of the horse-taming Trojans / will bring you to
    ransom a son

whom I might have seized / as a captive, I myself or
    another?

Or a young woman you want / whom you may have to
    make love

you yourself far apart, / to keep her? Ah no, shame it is

that a leader so plunge / into woe the sons of the
    Achaeans.

O milksops, O base, worthless things / O women and
    men now no longer,

homeward, back, with our ships / let us go, and here
    let us leave him,

here in the land of Troy, / to wallow in trophies, to
    know

whether or not we do also / count for something in
    war—

he who now upon Achilles / a man to him far superior

cast insults, and seized his prize, / holds it, took it
    himself.

Ah, but Achilles indeed / has a mind without passion,
    a weakling.

Or else, O son of Atreus, / this crime would have been
    your last.

At this point Odysseus suddenly appears beside Thersites,
rebukes him, and beats him. He crouches down and looks up

helplessly, wiping away his tears. The Achaeans, who just a little earlier approved of him, now turn their praise on the great Odysseus and cast scorn upon Thersites.

Such is Thersites: no sooner heard than silenced; alone, self-contained, yet giving full expression to the general predicament. The strong image is so conceived as to gather into itself the many currents of feeling running through the whole army—dismay at Agamemnon's outrage, war-weariness, longing for home. Rather then giving us a general survey, Homer has condensed in Thersites the general surge of countless grievances. On the other hand, he grows on us, becomes more and more convincing as a character, by absorbing the stresses of the time and making them his own.

Is Thersites, then, a rebel, a mutineer? Perhaps so, but only implicitly. He has no revolutionary ideas, but simply gives voice to a natural reaction, venting pent-up bitterness and hatred. Hence no general assertions, sweeping statements, or points of principle; he utters direct taunts, alludes to particular acts, placing emphasis on Agamemnon's greed rather than on injustice.

With his concrete sense of the occasion, Homer has drawn not a spokesman or a symbolic figurehead but a man who really stands up and cries out, speaking with the anguish of a victim and the conviction of an accuser. Hence the truth of the picture. We have a poetic objectivity which makes everything real and yet ideally significant. For the action and its moment are so realized that each actor seems to take an inevitable stance. Here is challenge, response, denouement—all as necessarily linked to one another as notes in the scale; and this interplay overshadows the relative stations of the men involved. Thersites is no hero, and yet we may sympathize with him rather than with Odysseus.

The sense of truth intrinsic to artistic perception here

opens the way to a broader view of human values, whatever the poet's intention or opinion may have been. For Homer is certainly no partisan of Thersites. He goes unusually far out of his way to give us a negative description of the man as a babbler, a troublemaker. Nonetheless, this man speaks out against Agamemnon in the same kind of language as Achilles uses, and he is, apart from Achilles, the only character that makes an incisive judgment both on Agamemnon and on the great quarrel that lies at the heart of the poem.

It could not have been otherwise. Homer naturally avoids complication, intrigue, any narrow or pointed characterization. Every character must grow from the broad outline of the action as it is perceived in its concrete development. It would have run counter to Homer's spirit had he made Thersites into, say, a schemer, liar, or contriver of plots. However much he might have been tempted to do so in the introductory lines, he could not follow it up. Thersites could only find life in the mainstream of the poem. For a few moments he plays the role of Achilles, standing out in the full dignity of his strength—and his weakness.

And this implicit sense of truth is carried even further. See how, when Odysseus attacks, the Achaeans who at first listened approvingly to Thersites turn mockingly against him. Yes, they say, Odysseus is a great man, Thersites a wretched babbler. They align themselves on the stronger side. The weakness, or the cowardice, of human nature comes to the fore.

So here is Thersites rather than the complaining thousands. Everywhere in Homer there is an urge to single out, highlight, individualize.

Hence the hundreds of personal names found in the *Iliad*, mostly heroes mentioned just before they are killed. For instance (*Il.* 6.20ff.), "Euryalus killed Desos and Opheltios . . . Astyalos was slain by warlike Polypoetes, Pidytes by Odysseus." At times something is said about their birth, as (6.22ff.): "He went against Aisepos and Pedasos, whom once the nymph Abarbarea bore to Bukolion"; or about their life, as (*Il.* 5.69ff.): "Meges killed Pedaios . . . whom divine Theano reared and loved."

These are little more than names. Through long stretches of the *Iliad* there are no characters to speak of. And yet the very fact that Homer mentions these names is highly significant. With deep insight, Jasper Griffin remarks: "Nothing is more characteristic of the poem; when we turn to the *Nibelungenlied,* or to the *Song of Roland,* or to the *Poem of the Cid,* we find nothing like this illumination of minor warriors who exist in order to be killed. In those epics what we have is, rather, a vast number of insignificant dead, without separate description or identity, whose simpler function is to make up a total for the great heroes of the day."

Here is another aspect of Homer's concreteness. There is no glorification of a central hero to whom countless, nameless victims are sacrificed; Achilles himself is seen for what he is, flesh-and-blood, vulnerable, exposed; and, by the same token, any other man is shown sharing the same existence, endowed with the same capacities and liabilities. Just as Achilles is fated to die young, so are many others; any young man is presented for a moment in his full vitality before meeting swift death. A resounding sentence such as "His eyes did dark death encompass and powerful fate" often tolls the solemn knell. The name alone is recognition of that silent human form which stands glowing for a moment, then falls.

In so vivifying and naming the dying warriors, the poet must have been engrossed with the thought of life and death. But art showed the way. Homer never tires of portraying action insofar as it brings into full evidence the might of animate form. Here was a central theme: a man's figure in the wonder of its articulate existence, whether at rest or moving, in advance or retreat. A wondrous figure, and yet so vulnerable. Death crushes it, and it exists no longer. So haunting and so familiar a thought must have blended with strong aesthetic perception. Hence, implicit in the particular name of a dying hero is a sense of that dignity which appertains to all life. Hence, more generally, the feeling of mortality which so permeates the *Iliad* and, in this respect, the sharp distinction between gods and men.

Aesthetic perception was thus essential to conceiving human values. First and foremost, we find the living image, rooted in nature, placed beyond the pale of good and evil, showing through its very existence the inherent innocence and worth of form. Then, growing articulate, the image becomes characterized more and more by the action; yet it retains its primal aesthetic appeal.

The mold of nature and a basic charm of form are inherent in all the Homeric characters. There are no downright villains, no idealized heroes; no superimposed reason or cause is allowed to spirit away the sheer force of nature. Nor, by the same token, is there any punctilious description: it would confer willfulness and bias upon the sweeping emotions Homer portrays. This is why all the Homeric characters have a broad, generous outline. Even the suitors in the *Odyssey*, whom we might expect to be treated as scoundrels, are only reviled in the minds of their opponents and are presented by the poet himself as simply pursuing their cause in the prime of manhood.

But here we are wandering beyond the notion of character. For Homer's image-making power is one with a sense of focus, position, form in nature itself. What stands out is the figure of a man or a woman seen against the background of the world as a whole, and thus all ethnic peculiarities are transcended by a sense of mankind, and mankind presented as part of nature. It is as though this universal outlook had been prompted by nothing more than Homer's keen perception of animate forms—by perceiving how any living organism, any vital shape, comes into full view, takes its place, attains its dignity in the realm of existence.

IV NATURE

I

A SENSE OF ANIMATE ENERGIES RUNS THROUGH HOMER'S
rendering of nature. His imagination was fired by any manifestation of life in its pertinent form. Such natural vitality
appeared first and foremost in the human figure. A hero's
action was, in this respect, the most striking natural phenomenon. For Homer does not take any act for granted: to rest,
to move, to clasp, to let go—such acts are, in Homer, points
of focus, moments that cannot be passed over but claim full
expression. Some essential part or organ of the body is at
work as if endowed with a power of its own, and a function
revealed which is as surprising as it is familiar. Quite apart
from the drift of the story, we linger over these natural instances of spontaneous activity.

When Ajax says in *Il.* 13.73ff.: "The spirit within my
breast is craving more strongly to fight; eager are the feet
below, eager the hands above," he highlights something that
is true at many points throughout the poems. Everywhere the
parts or organs of the body are presented as the source or
vehicle of an individual's faculties. Often they themselves are
the subject of the sentence rather than the individual person,
as if they were independent agents. It is, then, the feet that
step out, the hands that clasp, the eyes that look, the joints
and the knees that impart swiftness, as, for example, in
17.700: "As he [Antilochus] shed tears, the feet bore him away

149

from the battle, to bring the sad message to Achilles." (Compare *Il.* 5.885, 13.515, 18.148; *Od.* 15.555, 23.3; *Il.* 16.244, 23.627, 687; *Od.* 20.237, 21.202; *Il.* 23.477, 463; *Od.* 12.232; *Il.* 17.679, 14.286, 6.511, 9.610, 11.477, 22.388, 21.302.)

Especially the emotions are so presented as to shake the individual from within; and then the inner organ—in this case, the heart—seems to vibrate, to prompt, to spur on its own account. Thus Agamemnon tells Nestor (*Il.* 10.93ff.):

> In dreadful fear for the Danaans / I am, nor in me the spirit
> is still; I am in distress, / outward from me my heart
> is leaping away from my breast, / and the strong limbs tremble beneath.

(Compare *Il.* 1.103–04, 188–89, 3.33–35, 11.86–89, etc.) But, rather than any particular passage, it is the poet's usual language which constantly reminds us of seething powers at work within the human frame. We often find such phrases as "the spirit commands within me," "the heart broods within me," "he revolved in his midriff and soul," rather than simply "I wish," "I brood," "he ponders." The midriff, in particular, is a vital center wherein all manner of emotions, thoughts, and powers gather and quicken the inner life.

It does not matter who the character so presented may be. We touch upon life itself—the resilience of limbs, the pulsing of the senses, the effort which comprises all the might of a man. The heroes emerge out of a vital raw material. They are cast in the same basic mold, all framed—as Shakespeare would put it—in the prodigality of nature. Thus, in the *Iliad*, there is a pervasive sense of force more impressive, more significant than the prowess of any single hero. All share the same vitality intensified by the threat of imminent death. As in a fragment of Greek statuary, a clenching hand or a stepping foot suggests a nameless power which no amount of heroic glorification can match.

So, quite apart from the characters, we are aware of the very soil of existence in which they are rooted. A heart that throbs with excitement, a spirit that propels from within, hand and foot forthwith released into motion—here is energy and courage and purpose drawn, like breath, from nature's inmost core. It is as if we were presented with a deeper level of reality than that which we admire in the full-fledged characters. Lifeblood runs through the poems. It infuses the subject matter with its steadfast beat. Seen in this light, even the wrath of Achilles or the return of Odysseus might seem tenuous happenings arising momentarily on the surface of nature.

But Homer, of course, never refers directly to what so deeply affects his imagination. This sense of nature is fused with his representation of action. What stands out is always a crucial occasion that brings a human figure to the fore. In this broad perspective, we should look at the sheer physical impact of such occasions rather than read into them any ulterior motive. We see the moment materializing, suddenly bringing into the open and to full fruition a man's existential potentialities.

II

Homer's similes show that he views these human moments as natural phenomena and that they are therefore most relevant to his representation of nature. For why does a simile occur? Because a human act becomes so focused in itself and by itself that it inevitably removes us from the narrative element of the passage and, rather, impresses upon us its existential identity as an event taking place in its own right. As such, it stirs up analogies in the world of nature. It shifts our attention from the story to reality at large.

Take, in *Il.* 20.164ff., the simile that introduces Achilles into battle:

> And the son of Peleus / against him sprang as a lion,
> a ravaging lion: upon him / the men come striving to kill him,
> the whole of the village assembled; / at first he deigns not to heed them,
> forward he goes till perchance / one of the vigorous youths
> spears him; he draws himself up / gaping wide, and froth round the teeth
> gathers, while deep within / groans with its throbs his strong heart;
> with his tail, on the flanks, / and on the thighs, from both sides
> he smites, and the whole body / he then rouses up for the fight
> glaring; forth is he swept / with fury, perchance to kill
> one of the men, or to perish, / himself, in the thick of the fray—
> thus was Achilles stirred up / by his valiant spirit and might.

There are many other such animal similes in Homer (cp. *Il.* 12.41; 13.471; 16.156; 17.109, 133, 570, 742; 18.318; 21.573). They bring out an identity of movement in hero and animal. Homer does not say "as fierce as a lion" or "as swift as a horse," but "he *sprang* like a lion," he *ran* like a horse." This is to say that qualities or characteristics are not taken for granted but are seen in the act of realization, their actuality of position or movement. The human act, focused as it is, overflows into the animal. Being so singled out on its own strength, it ceases to be distinctive of this or that hero; it even loses its peculiar human connotations; it simply embodies natural vitality and power. Hence the simile summons up analogies, instances far removed from the human and yet endowed with the same impact. With his feeling for action in and by itself, Homer was able to do equal justice to both the human and the extra-human moment. He saw them as being on the same level of experience. He looked at nature with sympathetic eyes. See how, in the simile just quoted, the lion, just like Achilles, is possessed of a valiant heart and is carried away by the same kind of might (*menos*). And yet he does not need at all to be humanized: each act—the bracing up, the desperate lunge—is defiance in nature. The self-asserting challenge is at home everywhere. Spirit belongs to any animal, as well as to man (*Il.* 23.468, 16.468, etc.).

Or take *Il.* 6.505ff.:

> He rushed then through the town / relying upon swift-moving feet.
> As when a horse kept as stallion, / with barley well-fed at his manger
> breaking away from his fetters / runs stamping over the plain,
> and his custom it is / to bathe in the fair-streaming river;
> in glory he goes, and up high / he holds his head, while the mane
> flutters over his shoulders; / and, possessed of his splendor,
> nimbly his knees bear him on / to the haunts and pastures of mares;
> thus did Priam's son Paris / down from Pergamon's heights

> in his armour aglow, / like shining sun, take his stride
> rejoicing, and the swift feet / bore him on. . . .

Again an identity of movement both in the hero and the animal; the movement evokes swiftness, freedom, joy. Paris'
momentary well-being suddenly becomes more than human.
It exists in the galloping horse, the open spaces, the lovely
river, the outlying pastures. From the perception of a buoyant
human shape in motion we unwittingly pass to a whole scenery.

How is this effect achieved? The first clue comes with the
impression of Paris' moving feet:

> he rushed then through the town / relying upon swift-
> moving feet

And this first impression, after carrying us through the simile,
finally brings us back to the starting point:

> and his swift feet bore him on.

The image of the horse thus absorbs that of Paris and refracts
it upon us at the end. The same movement passes from shape
to shape. The magic touch leads us on without break, simply
lingering on points of solidity and resilience. These—the
horse's upright head, the waving mane, the shoulders, the
knees—are both sources of energy and focal elements of form.
We might think of the Parthenon frieze: how the bodies of
men and horses are stops in the same rhythm. Arching shapes
as if restrained for a moment and then released, curves that
inevitably compose a human or animal figure, motion that
cannot but run into its pertinent form—these figurations tend
to remove us from the ostensible subject matter and even
from any particular species, suggesting any shape-producing
or life-enhancing stress in the world of nature. A foot, a knee

thus acquires a resonance that lies quite beyond them; and yet, by being universally significant, they are themselves more real and true to life.

Other animal similes are more complex. They bring out a relation: animals opposing or supporting one another the way heroes do in battle. Among the most interesting are those in which animals are shown defending their young (*Il.* 16.259, 17.4, 133, 18.319; *Od.* 16.216, cp. 20.14).

Take *Il.* 17.133:

Then over Patroclus Ajax / put his shield as a cover
and stood out as a lion / that stands protecting his
    young:
as he leads out his brood, / out in the forest they meet
    him
the men that are hunting, and he / seethes with the
    might pent within him;
all the skin of his brow / comes down enclosing his
    eyes;
thus over Patroclus Ajax / over the hero was standing.

How often we find in Homer heroes defending a fallen comrade, trying to avenge him or save his body from the despoiling hand of the foe (cp. *Il.* 13.384ff., 402ff., 417ff., 581ff., etc.). The central theme of the *Iliad*—Patroclus slain, his body retrieved, the revenge of Achilles—finds its counterpart not only in many other human instances on the battlefield but also in the world of nature. What essentially emerges again and again is an act of defense or defiance for something naturally dear. No matter what the human complexities may be, through the similes the act becomes an awesome fact of nature. The very plot of the poem brings us back to a drama of universal proportions.

III

The fall of a dying man is, as we have seen, a constant theme of the *Iliad*. More than anything else, it has a striking effect. Homer does not elaborate upon it. He does not usually go into gruesome details. He simply lets it occur in its tragic simplicity. But such a fall again strikes analogies through the realm of nature. What is more awesome and impressive than the fall of a tree felled by foresters or shattered by a storm? Hence, again, the image-producing simile of a tree (cp. *Il.* 4.482, 13.178, 389, 16.482, 17.53, cp. 8.306).

Take 17.53:

> As when a man rears a shoot, / the flowering shoot of an olive
> up in a lonely place, / where a gush of water wells up,
> a lovely blossoming thing; / ever swirled it is by the gusts
> of breezes hither and thither, / luxuriant with whitening blossoms;
> but then a wind all at once / arriving with fullness of blast
> turns it up out of its pit, / stretches it down to the ground;
> so was the son of Panthhoos / Euphorbus-armed-with-the-ash-spear
> struck down by Menelaus, / and stripped by him of his arms.

The same fall, the same pathos, exists in the human and the vegetal world. We are given a momentary glimpse of natural scenery: a solitary spot, a flowering tree, winds. Just as we are spared any detailed description of Euphorbus' death, so we are barred from any detail of the place. Anything picturesque would be inconsistent with the tragic sense of crisis that occasions the simile. What we see is simply the tree in its blossoming vigor. It stands in splendid isolation. Water nurtures it, breezes sport with it, but, far from adding any distracting detail, these are light, effective touches which enhance the tree-image, quickening it with air in the foliage and sap at the roots.

We may compare a simile that has the same purport—but in this case, a flower, not a tree. In *Il.* 8.306, Gorgythion is hit by an arrow:

> Like a poppy he let fall his head / on one side—a
>   poppy in a field
> weighed down by burden of seeds / and by the
>   showers of spring;
> thus on one side did his head / recline, weighed down
>   by the helmet.

Is Gorgythion dying, swooning, or simply drooping? We are not told. The literal fact is not specified. All the more are we kept within the pure realm of form, position. A standing shape that reclines, a sagging stoop, a slackening outline: here is a world-wide pattern into whose visual contours we may read all failure, faintness, and anguish. Hence the clear-cut and highly significant image of the drooping poppy. The poet holds us to it. He does not allow for any explicit pathetic effect. But the implicit dramatic significance confers strong focus upon the flower, reducing all embellishment of detail and leaving us only an open field.

Elsewhere, it is the resistance of a hero which evokes a tree. In *Il.* 12.131ff., Polypoites and Leonteus are so compared:

> Both of them out in front / before the high-rising
>   portals

> stood as stand upon mountains / the oaks-whose-head-
> soars-up-high
> while against winds they resist / and rainstorms from
> day to day
> fixed to the strength of their roots / that beneath them
> stretch far and wide;
> thus the two of them relying / upon their hands and
> their strength
> resisted. . . .

A rock or cliff might be similarly evoked. Thus, in *Il.* 15.618:

> They held in a mass, / in compact array, like a rock
> a huge precipitous rock / on the verge of the white-
> foaming sea
> that resists the swift paths / of the vociferous winds
> and the waves swelling high / that against it come in a
> roar;
> thus Danaans held against Trojans / unflinching, nor
> did they flee.

Resisting oaks, a rock. We pass into the sphere of what is regarded as inanimate: a rock is not a living thing like an oak. And yet in this perspective it also becomes animate. It stands out, resists, endures, retains its shape and identity against the raging of the elements. It is a landmark in existence.

Like the human act that evokes them, these instances of nature are momentary, self-contained, solitary. They come and go in a flash. The dramatic impact is inseparable from the visual representation; hence there is no local, no regional interest. We have airy spaces, commotions of the elements, forms of existence, rather than any distinctive features of weather, climate, or territory. We have nature rather than landscape.

But how is it that this representation of nature is as precise as it is general, as vivid as it is typical. The reason again lies in the motivating element, the human act which so engrosses the poet that it imposes its own measure upon nature at large. For such an act is as unique as it is typical of itself and therefore universal. Thence these visions of nature draw their quality: they are strong, clear, and yet homeless. We see an animal or a tree surrounded by just enough space or air to give them life: the picture is memorable because it is so quickly resolved into an image.

IV

So far we have seen many individual human acts or states of being summon up analogies in nature. Elsewhere, and very often, the emphasis lies on a teeming mass. The sound, the glitter of arms, the mere sense of a living multitude produce the impression of an overflowing surge in nature. But, again, what prompts the simile is the impact of a single movement that emerges in clear and simple outline through the sheer volume of its manifestation.

Take, for instance, the rallying of the Achaeans in *Il.* 2.455ff.:

As when a ravaging fire / flares over a limitless forest
upon the top of a mountain / and the glare is seen from
    afar;
thus as onward they marched / up from their
    marvelous bronze
a glow flashing out, / through the air, ascended up to
    the sky.
And they went as do birds / on their wing in full
    swarm—

wild geese either or cranes / or swans-of-the-tapering-
  neck—

out on the Asian meadow, / on both the banks of
  Cayster;

hither and thither they fly / in the might of their wings
  taking joy,

with cries ever forward alighting, / and the whole
  meadow resounds—

thus of them many tribes / out of the ships and the
  tents

were pouring over the plain / of Scamander; thereunder
  the earth

gave out a terrible echo / to the feet of men and of
  horses.

And they stood by Scamander, / there on the
  blossoming meadow

numberless, as many as are / the leaves and flowers of
  spring.

And as when there are flies / in many swarms thickly
  flying

that all over a farmstead / of sheep are accustomed to
  roam

in the season of spring / when with milk are drenched
  all the pails;

so many arrayed against Troy, / so many long-haired
  Achaeans

stood in the plain. . . .

The massive movement of the Achaeans prompts these
similes, which contain both a sense of quantity and of life.
The idea of great numbers is given sensuous, quickening
expression. An unmeasurable glow emanates from fire burst-
ing out in a great mountain forest; an unbounded sense of

flight and converging movement comes from an alighting swarm of birds; an incalculably pullulating activity is conveyed by flies gathering in their favorite haunt. And each occurrence naturally brings along its own scenery, but a scenery condensed and simplified by the movement that claims it as its essential space. Only the mention of the Asian meadow and the river Cayster provides a local indication, unique in the poems. Is the poet telling us something he saw himself? If so, the glorious flight of birds so impressed him that he could not leave out the actual location. In any case, what predominates is the same decisive touch: the way the natural scenery is reduced to the measure of one instant vision, remaining what it essentially is and yet brought into intimate relation with the sweep of one vital movement. We might thus be tempted to read these similes by themselves, without their object of comparison, in which case we would have a celebration of nature in the plenitude of her manifestations.

Compare, in the same book (*Il.* 2.87):

As when forth go the swarms / of the bees thickly-
    flying
from the hollow of a rock / in relays ever fresh coming
    out;
and in clusters they fly / over the flowers of the spring;
hither and thither they appear / in the throngs of their
    flight,
thus of them many tribes / out of the ships and the
    tents
before the deep-sanded beach / strode along in their
    ranks. . . .

We have the same kind of flight as in the bird simile. It is a theme dear to Homer: movement instantly taking shape and freely expanding to find its place in nature. Here is a simple

insight yet seldom given its unaltered chance, so free of ulterior motive and purely poetical. Virgil, for instance, uses a
bee simile for quite a different purpose, to highlight the industry of the Carthaginians in building their city (*Aen.* 1.430):
"as bees at the beginning of summer . . . leading out their
young . . . or packing the liquid honey . . . or taking over the
load of the incomer . . . or warding off the drones. . . ." Virgil's intent is moral, social, and political. Homer would never
use such a simile. He does not see bees as models of human
industry but wonders, rather, at their marvelous thronging
flight out of a rock far into the meadows. Whereas Virgil
found room elsewhere for his poetry of landscape, Homer's
visions of nature are scattered everywhere throughout the
poems and his landscape is an essential breathing-space or
vantage ground.

Other similes of this massive kind are those of the sea,
conveying a movement wave upon wave (*Il.* 2.144, 209, 4.422,
13.795). Let us look at 13.795:

> And they went with the strength / of winds,
>   resembling the blast
> which underneath the thunder / of father-Zeus sweeps
>   to the plain
> and with marvelous din / blends with the brine,
>   wherein many
> blustering waves are spread out / over the wide-roaring
>   sea
> with curving whitening crest, / some forward and
>   others behind;
> thus the Trojans, some forward / arrayed and some in
>   the rear

with a sparkling of bronze / went in the wake of their
   leader.

This movement naturally finds its eminent theme in the wave
that arches itself and then breaks with a liberating clash on
the shore (cp. 4.422, 11.307–08). Such is the shape of a body
in motion when projected forward, ready to advance or attack. This moment of focus naturally excludes any generalized
picture of the sea. What remains is the motion, the sweep.

The same effect applies to a field of corn (*Il.* 2.148):

As when the West-wind stirs / a field of deep-ripening
   corn
briskly spurting upon it, / and presses bending the
   blades;
thus was the assembly stirred. . . .

We are all familiar with this fleeting effect: the grass of a field
touched and transfigured into wavelike appearance by the
scouring wind. Homer does not describe the field at all, but
gives us a shadow or a flash that makes it alive for a moment.

Compare, in *Il.* 7.63, a similar effect in a different sphere:

As at the touch of the West-wind / a ripple spreads
   over the sea
when a gust newly rises, / and the waters darken
   beneath it;
thus were seated the ranks. . . .

People sitting close to one another cease to be distinctive human shapes; they are fused into one extensive patch that
nevertheless quivers with life. In the same way, we may be
struck by the rippling dark mass of water. Again, as in the
case of the windswept field, there is no interest in details or
picturesque features. Nor do we have any general view. What

appears is a quickening moment in the waters, a tension, a condensation, a process that materializes and takes form—whether in the human sphere or in the sea.

The process of simplification, focus, and high relief is especially remarkable in these similes conveying a sense of multitudes, for the large quantity envisaged lends itself to description. A superficial composer might easily be tempted to expand on the number of birds or bees, telling us how they filled the air or completely covered their resting places. Or he might work up the effect of the sea-waves and bring in the general power of the sea. The taste for detail or exaggeration might here have ample scope. But not so in Homer. Like a great painter, he confers form, outline, rhythm and meaning upon the multifarious shows of things. The whole earth and sky and sea are unmistakably there; but a blossom, a wind, a ripple, a wave are so summoned up as to crystallize a high moment of life at their own climax and thus naturalize the human condition.

And this effect is achieved by the simplest of means, by the pure power of vision—vision not only receptive but active. Seeing is a faculty we all have; we see what our powers of vision let us see. But how often is this faculty used mechanically, thus becoming passive. The opposite is the case in Homer. With a master touch he instinctively leaves out the mere multiplicity of things and highlights those points of focus which respond to his sympathetic insight: at such points the taste of life conditions or prefigures the vision of nature.

V

We find, finally, the simile directly prompted by an emotion. Take the case of Nestor watching the routed Achaeans (*Il.* 14.16):

As when darkens the sea, / in its mighty expanse, with
a groundswell
in its foreboding of winds / that resound in swift-
sweeping paths,
and it stays as it is, / neither forward nor sideways it
rolls
until with manifest strength / down from Zeus comes a
gale;
even so the old man revolved / divided thoughts in his
mind.

Similarly, of Agamemnon (*Il.* 10.5):

As when he flashes with lightning, / of-fair-tressed-
Hera-the-lord,
working up a great storm / in wondrous fashion, or hail
or such snowfall as often / sprinkles the earth with its
flakes
or he fashions perchance / the jaws of sharp-piercing
war;
thus, as thickly, in his breast / Agamemnon gave out
his sighs
up from the depth of his heart, / and the midriff
trembled within him.

Of Penelope, listening to Odysseus who, disguised, gives
news of himself (*Od.* 19.204):

As the snow melts away, / upon a high-ranging
mountain
when it is thawed by the East-wind / after the West-
wind has poured it;
and, as it melts, from its source / the rivers run down
in fullness;

> so was she; her cheeks melted, / the lovely cheeks,
>   with her tears
> as she wept for her husband. . . .

And, in joyful sense, the Achaeans suddenly relieved (*Il.* 16.297):

> As when away from up high, / away from a great
>   mountain's summit
> a thick cloud is removed / by Zeus-assembler-of-
>   lightnings;
> all lit-up suddenly appear / the hill-tops and
>   furthermost headlands
> and valleys, while from the heavens / the infinite air
>   breaks out free;
> so did the Danaans take breath. . . .

We are so accustomed to drawing a line between the mental and the material, between spirit and body, that we may find it strange to see anguish likened to a storm, tears to melting snow, relief to a clearing after fog. But to Homer the resemblances came naturally from the way he viewed psychic processes. I have emphasized the concreteness of Homer's rendering of the emotions: just as a foot moves or a hand clasps, so does heart or spirit throb, quiver, spur. What may seem to us a disembodied process becomes a tangible event in its own right.

Hence the resulting representation of nature. Just as human sensations are natural phenomena, so do the commotions of the elements acquire human coloring. Some Homeric trace still remains when we say an "angry sky" or a "stormy temper" and, for instance, ascribe serenity both to the mind and to a day. But when we do so, we are either consciously using metaphors or are taking certain expressions for granted.

We hardly realize that wholeness that could make us see in a burst of passion and a peal of thunder two aspects of the same phenomenon. The easy metaphors prevent us from appreciating the dramatic impact of the occurrence itself.

Not so in Homer. That dark heaving of the sea, that silent pent-up power, that ground swell which keeps just below the breaking point, is a threat, a presentiment, a foreboding, as in someone who, on the eve of a final and reckless decision, does not yet know which way to turn. That fitful flashing of the sky, that sudden vehemence in the air, is like a seething inner ferment that makes the blood boil and the heart throb faster. That melting of snow and ice at the approach of spring, with its attending flow of water down the mountains, is a kind of liberation, as when too much grief or too much joy cannot but erupt in tears. And that cloud suddenly vanishing, that wide perspective suddenly opening up to our eyes, that transparent air at last revealing every shape and contour—is it not space and breath and freedom, is it not like release to a darkened mind?

On their own ground these visions of nature present a sense of life that is both human and extra-human. In Homer we find hardly any instances of the so-called pathetic fallacy, which consists in directly attributing to nature at large specifically human emotions and qualities. The reason lies in the degree to which people are seen as part of nature. For Homer, the gap between mankind and the other parts of existence is not as wide as it is for us; and so there is no need to bridge the gap, to restore the identity of life by humanizing animals or plants or the elements.

The Homeric similes thus always compare a human event to a natural phenomenon, not the other way round. We would never find in Homer a simile like the one in Virgil's *Aen.* 1.148ff., which compares a calming storm at sea to a tumultuous mob pacified by an eloquent orator. Homer would avoid any point of this kind. He would rather draw a simile from nature for the words of a greater speaker, as when Odysseus' words are "like flakes of snow that, in winter, course through the air" (*Il.* 3.222).

The natural phenomenon, in other words, is not narrowed down to a particular human sphere; it is the human act which is enlarged by the comparison. Hence the forthright, sweeping outline of Homer's scenery, as essential as the act which it mirrors. Virgil's treatment of the pacified mob is much more elaborate than any Homeric rendering of seawaves. Why? Because what counts in Homer is incisive position or movement rather than behavior, dramatic representation of form rather than description.

VI

Even when a Homeric simile develops at length, the same concise outline prevails throughout: we do not have additional details, but the direct pursuit of the same movement. For example, take *Il.* 12.278:

> . . . as with the snowflakes / densely falling on earth,
> when comes a day in the winter / and Zeus-the-wise stirs himself
> to let snow fall, unto men / showing the might of his shafts.
> The winds he then sets to rest / and steadily pours till he covers
> the peaks of the mountains up high / and afar the furthermost headlands
> and the plains blest with bloom / and men's fields richly tilled.

> Even where land meets the sea / it is spread, on
>   harbors and shores;
> but the wave with its touch / keeps it off, while each
>   other thing
> is all over encompassed, / when the storm of Zeus
>   presses on;
> thus from one side and the other / in dense array flew
>   the stones.

The similes concentrate within themselves all those features of nature which we find scattered throughout the
poems; for, even outside the similes, Homer never gives any
detailed account of places. It is thus difficult to establish any
topography—of Troy and its territory, for instance. What we
find are essential outlines that are universally valid: a city on
a hill, the plain below, the river Scamander, the sea, a mountain in the distance. But these suffice to give a sense of reality;
for, without describing them in detail, Homer constantly
marks their presence insofar as the action revolves around
them, in them, and beside them. The sea resounds at their
feet as the Achaeans pass by; wind-smitten Ilium rises before
them; from many-fountained Ida, Zeus observes the scene;
upon the plain the battle sways to and fro; the strip of land
between hill and sea is an essential breathing-space. As in
the similes, whatever landscape there is, gives bare and solemn outline to the action.

The *Odyssey* presents us with the same grand, sharp outlines. In a poem so concerned with wanderings through many
places we might expect a variety of landscapes. But no; it is
as if the similes of the *Iliad* were reflected in the essential
patterns of scenery which the story yields to our view.

Take, for instance, Odysseus sailing from Ogygia to the
land of the Phaeacians. There appear to him (*Od.* 5.279ff.):

                                            the shadowy mountains
of the Phaeacian land / at the part which to him was
    the nearest,
and it looked like a shield / upon the mist-colored sea.

There Poseidon stirs up a storm (5.291ff.; cp. 9.67, 12.313,
14.303):

                                              stirred up the blasts
of the winds from all sides, / and with clouds did he
    encompass
both the land and the sea, / night swept down from the
    sky.
Together the East-wind and South-wind / swooped,
    and the West-wind ill-blowing
and Boreas-born-of-the-clear-sky / rolling a great flood
    before him.

Then (313ff.):

                                              a wave swept him over
dreadfully falling upon him, / it spun the raft all
    around.
Far away from the raft / he fell himself, and the rudder
from his hand he let go, / the mast was broken in half
by the dread blending of winds / plunging on him in
    their blast.

He manages to get hold of the raft,

    and the great wave swept her on, / upon the flood,
        hither and thither;
    and as Boreas in Autumn / carries the tufts of the
        thistle
    over the plain, and thick / to one another they cling;

> Now was it the turn of the South-wind / to dash her
>   onto the North-wind,
> then again did the East-wind / give her up to the West-
>   wind's pursuit.

Finally, the sight of land close by (399ff.):

> He urgently swam and he strove / to step with his feet
>   on the land,
> When he was from it as far / as one might shout and be
>   heard,
> then did he hear the roar / of the sea upon crags, upon
>   rocks.
> For there splashed the great flood / against the banks of
>   the mainland
> in wondrous thundering roar, / and all was veiled in
>   the sea-spray.
> No harbors there were / for the ships, and no sheltering
>   places;
> but jutting cliffs on the water / and massive rocks and
>   sharp crags.

Odysseus swims along the coastline until he finds, at the
mouth of a river, a hospitable approach. Praying to the river-
god, he is received into the friendly waters, finally lands,
stoops to kiss the earth, and, on high ground, finds a place
of rest (476):

> under twin bushes
> grown up both from one stock; / an oleaster and olive;
> through them no, not a wind / with its might of damp
>   breath could blow
> nor could ever the sun, / shining, strike through with
>   its rays

nor could rain penetrate / in the depth; so thick did
   they grow
with each other entwined . . .

We are reminded of the similes of the *Iliad*. The same
sharp outlines are here, but they now constitute the actual
scene of the story. Nature encompasses Odysseus. It inevitably confronts him in his struggle to pursue his journey. It
is either foe or friend: there is no neutral ground. The natural
element always enters into a dynamic relation with the man;
hence the close kinship with the similes. For there is always
a moment of action—resistance or escape, a damning or saving moment—and this stress continually tends to oust any
detailed description. That mountain looming over the sea is
a beckoning promise; that wave sweeping over Odysseus is
like a warrior attacking him; those reefs and rocks are signs
of mortal danger; that river is a saving grace; those twin trees,
a place or recovery.

   Are, then, these features of land and sea only to be appreciated in terms of safety or danger? Far from it. And yet
it is Odysseus' hopes and fears that infuse them with such
strong relevance. A wave or a rock, because of its very threat,
is seen as a powerful shape; a distant shore, because of its
very appeal, becomes an entrancing vision. By being so pertinent to a specific moment in life, things strike both the senses and the imagination. The sense of form—and ultimately
of beauty itself—finds its source in an instinctive, vital response.

   We may appreciate the fact, then, that when Odysseus
lands at last we find no specific description of the newly discovered land but simply a welcoming river, a tree, and the
mother earth. It is as if Odysseus were entering the house of
a bountiful host. The river-god, none other than the river

itself, opens the way. Henceforward any feature of the landscape that is mentioned is a vantage-ground, a stopping place,
a point of focus. Human need singles out of the general scenery one element, one distinctive landmark which, on that
very strength, assumes an independent identity and grows
in the imagination.

Take the twofold tree. Why not have, rather, a description
of a forest within whose thickets Odysseus might find shelter?
The reason is that any yearning loves form, any boon or delight we seek becomes most vital and poignant by being concentrated in one image. So, rather than the vague general
atmosphere of a forest, there is this single plant which, in a
clearing, stands out in itself and by itself, as dear to Odysseus
as the fig tree to which he clung on the rock of Charybdis
(*Od.* 12.432). Neither wind, or rays of the sun, or rain could
penetrate its branches, the poet tells us; and it is as if all the
shelter and quiet and stillness of the world's forests were here
concentrated in one spot. Similarly, we often find in Homer
a wave rather than the sea. Hence a singular effect: the startling plenitude of what is most familiar.

In order to be effective, a form or image must be per-
spicuous. It must give strong expression to what is already
familiar. Any curious or complicated structure may be remembered and punctiliously described, but it will fail to have the
incisive effect of a simple, clear-cut image: hence, in the Homeric similes, the recurrent view of a tree or a wave. Unusual
occurrences are likened to what is usual, not the other way
round, as might be the case of a composer trying to impress
rather than touch on the truth of things.

Hence a scenery which is as appealing to our sense of
recognition as it is singularly simplified and condensed. It is
so throughout the wanderings of the *Odyssey*—on the one

hand, the extension of far, legendary regions and, on the
other, a fundamental uniformity. Everywhere we catch fleeting sight of what might be a shelter, an appealing place of
rest, or a formidable, beetling cliff. The entrance to Hades is
characterized by "a narrow strand and the grove of Perseph-
one, tall poplars and willows that shed their fruit yet unripe";
on the island of the Cyclops meadows come into view and, at
the mooring spot, a spring ringed, again, by poplars; steep
cliffs surround Aeolus' island; from a height, Odysseus sees
smoke rising from Circe's dwelling in the midst of a forest;
Scylla appears as no more than a huge rock whose gray, misty
surface wearies Odysseus' eyes. Even such extraordinary
beings as Circe or the Cyclops live in a familiar setting and,
apart from their mythical features or faculties, they cannot
but lead ordinary human lives—the Cyclops as a shepherd,
Circe weaving and singing.

Just as in portraying people Homer shuns any narrow
peculiarity or ethnic trait and custom, so it is with places far
and near. Even so central a place as Ithaca is never described
in any detail (cp. *Od.* 4.606, 9.27, 13.238). To Menelaus, who
offers horses to Telemachus, the latter replies (4.606):

> Ithaca, no, does not have / wide running places or
>   meadows—
> goat-pasturing land and more lovely / than one that is
>   breeder of horses.
> For none there is of the islands / that's fit for horses or
>   meadows,
> none on the face of the sea; / so is Ithaca more than all
>   others.

Telemachus is right. Ithaca is the essence of all other islands.
Anyone sailing through the Greek seas naturally singles out
a high-rising mountain, cliffs, and beaches; and, scanning

closer, a town, a spring, tilth, and vineyard. No wonder that
scholars have shown the same certainty in either identifying
Homer's Ithaca with the modern one or in denying such an
identification. Yet Ithaca has the distinction which life confers
to what it knows. The features mentioned—the great mount
Neritos, the rugged slopes, the famous spring, the cave, the
mooring places—may be no different from others in other
places; but they are fixed in the mind of the characters, they
are thought of, loved. Hence Ithaca acquires an individuality
of its own. It becomes a mental image.

How significant it is that Odysseus does not at first recognize his Ithaca. Athena, we are told, altered the view of

> the long-stretching paths / and the ever-harboring
>   havens
> and the precipitous cliffs / and the burgeoning trees.
>
> [*Od.* 13.195–96]

But this failure to recognize is not unnatural. Odysseus, suddenly put ashore there by the Phaeacians, has seen numberless islands in his wanderings. Is this another such island?
His idealized memory of Ithaca needs time before it converges
with the place itself. Then, when recognition does come, each
feature will suddenly fall into place. And thus it happens. All
at once Odysseus is moved, he kisses the soil and utters his
prayer to the cave of the nymphs opening up before him. Yes,
here is a land like many others; but when such strong feeling
permeates the visual sense at a point of recognition, sweetness and beauty permeate the vision. "Goat-pasturing land,"
says Telemachus, "but more lovely than one which is breeder
of horses." No patriotism, no provincialism here, nor any
pure aesthetic sense, but a warm, strong perception of things
intimately known and thus responsive to a deep need of our
being. And here, certainly, is a source of beauty.

VII

What about beauty itself? What of nature simply contem-
plated, admired, enjoyed for its own sake? Is there no trace
of this direct appreciation in Homer?

I must refer, again, to Homer's concreteness. We do not
find in the poems any particular effect created for its own
sake, abstracted from the event which actually produces it.
No more than he would describe a person's behavior apart
from an actual occasion does Homer render a scenic effect
apart from single shapes actually coming into view and affecting the action. No sense of atmosphere is pursued beyond
the boundaries of what can be clearly seen and touched—as
when, say, the slanting rays of the setting sun hold all things
in the enchantment of their glow.

We call "beautiful," "sublime" any effect that so spirits
us away from the actual presence of a thing and transfers us
into a world of its own. In Homer there is no such abstraction.
Beauty is not idealized in itself. It is intrinsic to the relation
which obtains between the viewer and the object viewed.
Rather than beauty, we have a concrete effect of awe and
power. Here is something that takes place, happens, encompasses the senses of the beholder or participant. No question
of merely looking objectively, observing or appreciating details; no, it is as if a thing so looked upon exerted upon anyone
seeing it the power of its presence.

We may be given a clue by Odysseus looking at Nausicaa
in wonder and likening her to the sacred palm tree he once
saw in Delos by Apollo's altar (see above, p. 100). "Awe seizes
me as I look," he says; and the sense of loveliness blends with
awe as if the divine quality of the tree imparted to the girl
herself something godlike, as if beauty and deity were but

aspects of the same reality. Religious feeling thus sets in, a mysterious power making its way at a pertinent spot and moment, influencing the action.

Beauty is thus caught by the wing. It comes in dramatically. It is not a theme of description. Even where the view extends at length, we are made to feel its impact. Any charm of detail is superseded by the sense of an all-encompassing presence.

Such is the case of Hermes looking at the environs of Calypso's cave (*Od.* 5.63ff.):

> Around the cave was a grove / in full growth, in full
>   bloom—
> alder and poplar were there / and the sweet-scented
>   cypress.
> It was the wont of birds, / long-wingéd birds, to roost
>   there
> owls and with them the falcons / and the chattering
>   sea-crows
> that roam over the waves / and love the haunts of the
>   sea.
> Right on the spot stretched out / upon the deep hollow
>   cave
> a garden-vine in its youth, / with all its clusters in
>   bloom.
> Springs in a row, four of them, / flowed with radiance
>   of water,
> running near one another, / their course turning hither
>   and thither.
> Meadows lay there about them, / soft, with violet and
>   parsley
> blossoming; and at that spot / even a god, if he came,

rapt in wonder would gaze / and feel delight in his
   heart.
Standing there the god wondered. . . .

Or Odysseus looking at Alcinous' garden (*Od.* 7.114):

There were trees standing high / grown to fullness, in
   bloom—
pear- and pomegranate-trees / and apple-trees splendid-
   fruited,
there were figs in their sweetness, / there were
   burgeoning olives.
Of them all not a fruit / is ever lost nor it fails,
be it summer or winter, / perennial; but ever more
the breath of the West-wind brings / one to light, the
   other to ripeness.
Pear upon pear waxes mellow / and so does apple on
   apple,
and cluster of grape upon grape, / and likewise fig
   upon fig.
There for him also, most rich, / a vineyard had struck
   its root.
One part of it was warmest, / placed on ground that
   was level
ever dried by the sun; / some of the grapes do they
   gather,
others they press into must. / In front are clusters still
   green
with blossoms only just shed, / while others are turning
   ruddy.
Garden-plots well arrayed / stretch out at the end of the
   orchard,
flowering beds of all manner / shining forever in their
   glory.

> And two springs are there running: / one over the
>   extent of the orchard
> is scattered, whereas the other / under the court's outer
>   threshold
> goes to the high-built house, / and from it the people
>   draw water.
> Such in Alcinous' home / were the splendid gifts of the
>   gods.
> Odysseus standing there wondered. . . .

It is significant that, in both instances, the scenery requires a
beholder. It must have its impact. There must be an actual
point of contact for the representation to have its place. Each
feature stands on its own, and it is the wondering gaze of
Hermes or Odysseus that binds everything together.

What is the quality that so engrosses the beholder? What
various elements does this scenery have in common? What
kind of beauty is this?

There is, first of all, a fullness of being. Each thing is thus
just what it is, and yet it participates in a general amplitude
of life. What strikes us is the exuberant vegetation, the rich
growth. It diffuses into a general quality while being integrated with the actual form of each plant mentioned. The
atmosphere or spirit of the place cannot be separated for one
moment from the tangible presence of what is there.

How is such a vivid yet objective effect achieved? No such
impression would be ours if we merely stopped and admired
the rich fertility of a piece of ground. Homer does not take
this exuberance for granted or simply treat it as a theme for
praise; the exuberance is caught in the act. A garden-vine in
its youth stretches over the cave, pears wax mellow, grapes
redden—all is driven to fruition by an inner force. Hence no
curious observation of charming details but everywhere a

restless activity which is in itself a source of wonder. The flight of birds, the flow of waters further this sense of movement and life.

It is remarkable that the words *beauty,* and *beautiful* are not used for this scenery—no more than they are applied to the waves, rocks, mountains, and trees of the similes. We find instead many words for "blossoming," "flourishing." But the sense of beauty comes from the admiring gazes of Hermes and Odysseus. After crossing the wastes of the sea, it is as if they rediscovered the earth's bounty all concentrated in one spot. Natural beauty is thus a welcoming hand as well as a delight to the eye. It is lost in a more pervasive reality yet sharply realized at a decisive moment of impact.

VIII

Homer, on the other hand, frequently calls a man-made object "beautiful" insofar as it is well-constructed, perfectly fitted to its function, or brought to perfection through the harmony of its parts. What is the corresponding quality in nature, in plant or animal? It is similar, we may suppose, yet far more complex, baffling, and mysterious. For here at work is a power that makes a plant or animal what it is: a capacity to be, to live, to grow, to attain full vitality.

The word *beautiful* in its ordinary sense of "well-made" or "good to look at" might thus seem inadequate to the larger sphere of nature. What comes to the fore in Homer is the idea of a divine manifestion. Such a sense of the divine need not surprise us. We are tuned to it by Greek myth and by our own poetic feeling. Homer, who in the swift dramatic development of the poems leaves little room to nymphs and nature-gods, is all the more inclined to portray directly the animate force running through nature at large, letting a divine power implicitly permeate the imagery itself.

It is significant that the scenery of Calypso's cave and of Alcinous' garden (the two instances that come closest to "landscape") is in both cases on divine ground: Calypso is a goddess and the Phaeacians are close to the gods. We are expressly told that the trees and vines of Alcinous were a gift from the gods, hence the amazing vegetation. And yet for Homer nature is divine in its own right. His picture does not go beyond the boundaries of what is natural. That swift ripening in Alcinous' garden is still possible in a propitious climate; the luxuriance around Calypso's cave is the kind that any happy island may be blessed with. The full-blown moment—whether in a hero's effort or in a plant's growth—suggested a god. Homer did not have to seek any such miraculous place as the garden of the Hesperides.

Beauty in action, one might say; or, rather, a mysterious power at work in the perceived object and drawing the beholder into its own sphere. The religious element emerges more clearly in the cave of the nymphs at Ithaca, near which the Phaeacians land sleeping Odysseus (*Od.* 13.96ff.):

> A harbor of Phorkys exists, / Phorkys-old-man-of-the-
> sea
> out in Ithaca's land; / two jutting headlands upon it,
> sheer precipitous cliffs / on the harbor-mouth crouching
> down,
> keep off the violence of winds / and the mighty waves
> which they blow
> out in the main, while inside, / without any cable are
> stayed
> the well-benched ships when they come / within the
> space of their mooring.
> There at the head of the harbor / grows an olive-with-
> tapering-leaves,

and, beside it, a cave / a lovely cave all enshadowed,
a sacred place of the nymphs / who are called Naiads
  by name.
Therein basins are hollowed / and voluminous bowls
worked in the stone, into which / honey is stored by
  the bees,
and there are looms made of rock, / very high, upon
  which the nymphs
are ever weaving their robes, / sea-purple—a wonder to
  look at;
therein ever flow waters. / A twofold entrance leads to
  it—
one on the North-wind's side, / and down it men may
  descend,
but on the South-wind's side / it is for the gods; nor do
  ever
men come in by that way, / it is the path of immortals.

No rendering of any picturesque effect here. The spell of the cave at once takes fullness of form, and form that suggests activity: bowls, looms. Here is nature's art at work, and by whose hand but that of the nymphs to whom the cave is sacred? But the nymphs themselves are nowhere to be seen, nor are the gods whose entrance is hidden from human eyes. All the more there is a divine effluence from the cave itself. Beauty is fostered by awe.

The very appearance of the cave is kept in focus by religious feeling. For there is a divine extra-human ferment in the activity with which the cave is alive: in the work of the bees, the weaving of the nymphs, the flow of waters; and the presentation of these activities, which are one with the actual shape of the rock, excludes all description of incidental details. The mysteries of the cave thus give it its form. There is no separate account of the place on the one hand and of the presiding god on the other. No, the wholeness is inextricable, making each feature intrinsic to the spot and yet suggestive of a wider reality. Hence the strong, memorable effect of the picture.

But why is the cave there at all? Again, as elsewhere in Homer, the reason lies in the concrete impact of any object that is singled out. To returning Odysseus the cave embodies the genius of the place. No wonder that he turns to it in worship. Here is a vision that delights the eye and, at the same time, a spot as awesome as an oracle, as comforting as home. The effect is an enveloping one. Here is beauty, but enshrined by the attending pieties.

Elsewhere, though rarely, we are removed from any human environment to a place where only gods are present, and nature, in sudden celebration, seems to express recognition of their presence. Again there is beauty, but it is a natural phenomenon shot through with feeling. The effect is brief, flash-like.

Such is the case when Poseidon rides the waves in *Il.* 13.27ff.:

> And he drove over the waves; / the fish leapt under his impact
> out of the depth all around, / they failed not to know their lord;
> and in joy the sea clove apart. . . .

Nowhere else in Homer is a natural element so imbued with human emotion. The presence of the god is decisive. It is magnetic. It imparts a sympathetic movement to the waters. Hence the pervasive range: through the leaping, dancing fish, the sense of life penetrates the sea itself, which erupts in a shudder of joy. The moment is almost mystical; and yet it is kept within the bounds of Homeric form. The sea-waves of the similes, arched like human bodies in motion, pointed the way. The sea is caught in one immense wave, the animate stress is the same but enlarged and more penetrating. We have a sudden movement, no general picture.

Another instance is the love-scene between Zeus and Hera (*Il.* 14.346ff.):

> So he said and in his arms / he clasped her, the son of
>   Cronus;
> beneath them the earth divine / put forth new-
>   blossoming grass
> and the dewy lotus-flower / and the crocus and
>   hyacinth
> deep-petaled and soft / which lifted them up from the
>   ground.
> Therein they lay and upon them / they put a raiment of
>   cloud
> beautiful all of gold, / and shining dew-drops fell on
>   them.

Just as in the waters beneath Poseidon's feet, here we see a heaving movement of the earth. The powers of generation and growth come to a head, break out at a point of concentration and lift up the divine pair, as if to participate in their act of love. Interestingly enough, the word *beautiful* is reserved for the golden cloud the gods wear as if it were a robe and therefore in the objective sense in which it is often applied to man-made things. As for the rapturous event, it defies any qualification. Everything is motion, action, swift development, and full fruition. If beauty is a consummation in nature, here we have beauty in the making. Again there is no room for detail, no particular delightful spot begging to

be described. It is, rather, the swelling movement that acquires a shape. All charm lies hidden in the awesome manifestation of an encompassing power.

IX

Homer's representations of nature, as we have seen, are
as brief as they are concrete, in that they are always intimately
related to the unfolding action. Hence a bareness and simplicity that critics might ascribe to a certain stage in artistic
development and sensibility. It is thus urged that the ancient
Greeks in general, and Homer in particular, do not really
present us with any picture of landscape in the modern sense.
What they admired, it is said, was a rich fruitful land; they
were horrified by rocks, rugged ground, unapproachable
mountainous landscapes. For the same reason, those critics
might add, they could hardly have entertained the idea that
a storm was beautiful.

But the passages I have quoted, especially the similes,
tell us different. Many of them depict stormy skies and rugged
places. That Homer does not call this scenery "beautiful" or
does not explicitly praise it is irrelevant. What matters is the
vitality and power of the representation prompted by a strong
sense of the analogy between human actions and natural phenomena; and here surely lies the ultimate source of what appears beautiful in nature even in the wildest sense.
Commotions of the sky reflect emotions of the heart; arching
waves universalize a movement of which we are most intimately aware in our own bodies; a crashing tree dramatizes
a plight which also has its human form.

Homer's representation of nature hardly concerns any
question of taste characteristic of a certain age. What matters,
rather, is a sense of truth that produces beauty—how it is
discovered, brought out, expressed. The human eye naturally

gives a human tinge to what it sees—hence the warmth and intimacy of the vision. At the same time, however, the sense of movement, position, body, form, while so intrinsically human, appears to have a universal relevance on the face of nature. For Homer this realization came in the powerful focus on single instances. A resilient foot suddenly implied, for him, a body in motion and thus an advancing wave: movement embodied and body productive of movement. Or a standing then falling hero evoked, in the same way, a thriving, upright plant suddenly dashed to the ground. These are no figures of speech, not pertinent illustrations thought out for certain passages. The imagery of the similes finds its source in Homer's perception of nature in general, which is why it exists even outside the similes. Any mountain, rock, field, orchard, or tree is not taken for granted or displayed as a descriptive theme; it is, rather, a momentary presence that meets the eye or attends upon the action, a vantage-ground to human or animal life. No account of picturesque or interesting features; each spot seems to occur where it is, taking on dramatic evidence, living its moment even though it may be thought to be eternally present.

In such a portrayal of nature the sense of beauty is perhaps as yet unaware of itself. It is nevertheless present at the roots. It lies in the positive effect of so apprehending life in the full impact of form—in such central instances as make us see, even in a rock, a moment of exposure and resistance. This is why Homer's natural scenery is so simple and yet so haunting. Like an absorbing musical theme, it fills the imagination. It is as if the pulse of life running through the poems persisted in taking the forms most responsive to it. The olive tree of the Euphorbus simile, for instance, is akin to the one standing at the harbor mouth of Ithaca and to those in Alcinous' garden. So Thetis speaks of Achilles as a young shoot that soon must die, so Nausicaa is a blossom going to the dance.

A recurring theme rather than variety of description and, therefore, as we have seen, the grand, simple outlines of earth or sea. Here, more than ever, does an appealing vision oust any incidental point of interest or distracting multiplicity. Any local characteristic recedes. We might be anywhere in the world—wherever movement, position, or form has vital meaning.

A focus so strong and yet so universally applicable is eminently poetic. Homer's treatment of nature is the same, in this respect, as that of all great poetry in all ages. The storm in *King Lear*, for instance, or the island landscape of *The Tempest* could be anywhere. When Caliban says (*Tempest* 3.2.129–30): "Be not afeard. This isle is full of noises, / sounds, and sweet airs, that give delight, and hurt not," does he not express in terms of sound or air that vital spell which the island of Calypso presents in its vivifying growth? The obvious differences should not blind us to an essential poetic quality which the two passages have in common. For both exude an appeal that speaks to the senses. It tends to expunge or at least reduce any description of local details. And yet both places come alive because of the very fact that pervasive qualities are focused in them so strongly.

X

Homer's conciseness in rendering nature is what we should expect to find in a composition made up of action scenes that closely follow one another from moment to moment. Nature is given its place in the interstices the style affords.

Such is the case in the similes which, far from complicating the narrative, do no more than highlight the moment of action by letting it reverberate in the world of nature. This fullness gives power to the flow. The increased volume comes from the intrinsic significance of what is happening, not from any digression.

Other occasions, we have seen, are those in which a character arrives at a certain place: Odysseus at Alcinous' palace, Hermes at Calypso's island. Even the landing in Scheria is of the same kind: the river and the twin trees receive Odysseus as if he were a newly arrived guest. Again we have perspectives that open up most briefly—not by way of introduction, but to highlight things coinciding with the act of arrival and giving it visual evidence, especially where such an arrival is (as in the cases mentioned) a turning point. The view of the beholder or his actual step is never kept out of sight.

We might compare the many flashes of nature that mark the spot where anyone stands or goes: "they were enclosed into the deep-flowing bright-eddying river" (*Il.* 21.8); "he sat on the peak of many-ridged Olympus" (*Il.* 1.499); "they came to many-fountained Ida mother-of-beasts" (14.283). The sea is especially frequent: "sailing over the wine-colored sea" (*Il.* 7.88, cp. *Od.* 1.183, etc.); "she rose from the white-foaming sea" (*Il.* 1.359, cp. 13.352, etc.); "a ship out in the mist-colored sea" (*Od.* 8.568, cp. 5.281, etc.); "stepping out of the violet sea" (*Od.* 5.56, cp. *Il.* 11.298)—all instances that simply underline a point of movement or rest, but have a cumulative effect. On their strength we might recompose a shimmering, ever-changing vision of the sea. Nowhere do we find what we might call a seascape, however. The sea, rather, is always implicitly present. From many scattered points it infuses into the poems a sense of free, fluid spaces.

No extended description of landscape or seascape (or of anything else) could find room in Homer's style. The poems move swiftly. The dramatic momentum brooks no delays. If

NATURE   189

there is anything which, from a narrative point of view, we
may call a digression—Nausicaa at the river-mouth, for instance, or Hera and Zeus on Mount Ida—it forthwith ceases
to be a digression and becomes an event in its own right,
assuming the same rhythm as any other part. The heartbeat
of the poem will not have it otherwise. It imparts its throb to
continuous moments of the action, regardless of subject matter: scenery cannot help but participate in such moments so
conjured up.

Even when the material might seem to be intractable, the
effect appears to be the same. In the pictures of Achilles'
shield, for instance (Il. 18.483ff.), where we might expect description to gain the upper hand and draw the poet away from
his forthright path. But no; the treatment is again rapid. At
no point do we lose the sense of Hephaestus' hand actually
at work: "he made upon it the earth," "in it he made two
cities of men," "he set there a soft fallow-land." One thing
after another suddenly emerges into existence. The very fact
that each scene is a new one, freshly arising without any
pointed connection with those that precede or follow, is due,
at least in part, to the way the poet does not ever let us forget
the fashioning hand, the inventive moment. It is not so where,
as on Aeneas' shield, each scene is part of a greater whole
and stresses a historical or moral point. In Virgil (Aen.
8.626ff.), Aeneas surveys and admires the completed work;
in Homer, we see it taking shape upon the anvil.

Hence a terse, uncontrived art in Homer's Hephaestus,
as if the immediacy of representation were prompted by the
subject matter itself. His theme was unconstrained by any
partial interest, being none other than life itself (peace and
war, the seasons with their associated human tasks), and thus
he could give free rein to his imagination. But how else could
he do so except by condensing that scenery which the poems

themselves have made familiar? What ties the scenes on Achilles' shield to one another is thus a mode of perception that brings us back to Homer's sense of nature. Much that can be found in the similes or in sundry particulars of the *Odyssey* now emerges in a different context. Here is dark soil turned by the plough-share; here is a path trod by vintagers, leading into a vineyard heavy with grapes; here are harvesters sheaving corn and then resting under an oak; here are oxen walking to their pastures "along the murmuring stream, by the flickering reeds." Each spot is no sooner mentioned than it is filled with life, life no sooner envisaged than fixed to a pertinent spot.

My general approach to Homer's sense of nature does not fit in with the guidelines of much contemporary or recent scholarship. The prevailing view is that we have here, as usual, traditional material; and this assumption, whether right or wrong, is so strongly entertained that it often overshadows any aesthetic appreciation of the material itself.

Thus the scenery of the similes has long been presented as the poet's "stock-in-trade"—that is to say, a store of ready-made specimens to be used where convenient. Similarly, according to the theories of oral composition, the similes are no more than ornamentation: the singer expands his theme, enriches it with what devices the technique of oral composition affords; he knows beforehand that battle scenes require a certain kind of simile, that instances of arrival and departure require an elaboration of place. What again emerges is the notion of something ready-made, usable or disposable according to circumstance.

By thus taking for granted the perceptual process, these theories merely emphasize external features of composition and production. As a result, the poetic content is kept separate from the actual perception of reality; and the sense of truth in the representation of nature is either ignored or considered a detail of compositional talent.

But we can hardly do justice to Homer's rendering of nature without a feeling of how it is prompted by a vision of things—quite apart from whether we posit a tradition or an individual genius. What matters, ultimately, is the imaginative source: see how description always yields to realization from instance to instance; see how real, visual, and tangible is each place that comes into range. Any scenery is summoned up directly through the very fact of moving in, going to, or being in a certain place. Calypso's island opens up before Hermes as he steps from the sea; the very space of a hero's attack or resistance or fall evokes the beast's den in the forest or a tree's place on a mountain-top—all cases in which a body's position or movement strikes the imagination at one and the same time as the place touched. Ground to stand on, breathing-space, vantage point, widening prospect that meets the eye—the warm, vital sense of these things lies at the source of what we appreciate as natural beauty.

Places come alive through moments of action; moments of action find solidity in their pertinent places: here, nature has the concreteness of immediate experience. Such a form of representation is in harmony with everything else in Homer. For the facts that the action of each of the poems lasts only a few days, that these days frame salient instances of life from moment to moment, that as a consequence the characters dramatically pursue their career through existence—all attune us to rapidity of outline and avoidance of long-drawn-out description. Hence the flashes of the similes, the sudden views that rush to meet the eye. Here is poetic thought rather than compositional technique.

V AGE AND PLACE
OF HOMER

I

THE VERY GLORY OF THE ILIAD AND THE ODYSSEY HAS CON-
tributed to obscuring all records of the poet himself as a man
who lived in a definite time and place. The problem we are
faced with is thus that of establishing where, when, and how
the poems originated.

That they are the earliest extant remains of Greek literature is clear. Callinus and Archilochus refer to Homer as
early as the seventh century; the earliest figurative paintings
on Greek vases reproduce what seem to be Homeric scenes;
classical Greece placed the poems at the fountainhead of its
civilization. But the poems themselves seem to prove their
own antiquity. They give the impression of being at the
threshold of the age that ushered in ancient Greece. There is
in them a dawning sense of things to come, suspense between
a mythical past and a historical future. The Phaeacians, for
instance, live close to the gods, and yet their city—with its
agora, temple, and harbor—might be the Miletus of later
times. Troy, on the one hand, might seem a typical Mycenaean citadel with its large royal palace, while its temple of
Athena, the robe-offering women, and the individual houses
of Hector or Paris might make us think of Athens itself. Agamemnon and Odysseus are kings of the Mycenaean type, and
yet their powers are questioned, opposed, endangered as if

192

we were witnessing the incipient struggles of the early city-state. The heroes have their definitive say, but assemblies exist and the voice of the people makes itself felt.

In a more general sense, everything appears fluid. There is a hint of the existence of social classes (e.g., *Il.* 2.198), but class distinctions are nowhere emphasized. Slaves exist but no large slave population. Women do not seem to participate in banquets but are free to appear anywhere else. There is, of course, an awareness of the Greeks as a distinct nation but no one name to call them by, no notion of "barbarians," no settled national entity. There is a sense of mystery about the unexplored regions of the western Mediterranean and yet (especially in the *Odyssey*) the inquisitive eye, the exploring spirit, the trading instinct. Argos, Sparta, Mycenae, Pylos are no doubt important centers enriched by the glory of a legendary past, and yet they are not especially honored; they are simply particular cities out of many the world over (see the Catalogue of Ships, *Il.* 2.494ff.). There is no exclusive loyalty to any one place, no glorification of a certain king or country. The eye wanders near and far; the point of focus is the human action, the human situation, wherever it may be.

II

These signs point to a period later than the Mycenaean age and earlier than the full development of the early Greek city-states. For, whereas Mycenae lay at the mythical source of the poems, early Greece can be felt in the spirit which informs them.

We may give here a few traditional dates: fall of Troy 1184–83 B.C.; Dorian migration 1104–03; Ionian migration 1044–43. For what they are worth, these dates provide a reference point. They present us with a kernel of truth. For, as the archaeologists tell us, the great Mycenaean centers were destroyed in the twelfth century B.C.—presumably by the Dorians, that last wave of Greek settlers (Dorian Invasion) that ousted or subdued those who had preceded them, whence the massive migration of Ionians and Aeolians across the Aegean and their resettlement both on the coast of Asia Minor and the islands. The war of Troy was thus the last major Mycenaean exploit before the destruction of Mycenae.

Homer, then, lived after 1000 B.C. The date has been narrowed down by archaeological and linguistic evidence: for instance, according to T. B. L. Webster, the decorated shields of Achilles and Agamemnon point to the eighth century, while vowel contractions and loss of the *digamma* (or *w* sound) are assigned by E. Risch to the same age. The eighth century appears a suitable date from a general point of view: if the migrations took place in the eleventh to tenth centuries, we should allow for a period of settlement and development.

But what evidence is there that Homer was a Ionian? There is the strong traditional claim of Chios as his birthplace. There is the evidence of language—Ionian dialect with a mixture of Aeolian (Aeolia and Ionia were contiguous). There is— last but not least—the evidence of some of the similes which, we may suppose, reflect the poet's own experience: the Asian meadow and the river Cayster (*Il.* 2.461), the winds coming from Thrace (9.5), or sweeping the Icarian Sea (2.145).

III

Did Homer, then, compose the poems in eighth-century Ionia? The very question has been made to sound absurd ever since the "Homeric question" was raised some two hundred years ago and, on the assumption that no writing existed in Homer's day, the name of the poet became a mere designation for a whole genre or for whoever put together, in their present form, pieces of varying provenance and date. The same question might seem equally absurd today when, according to the prevailing theories of oral composition, Homer is indeed allowed to have existed, but only as the ultimate spokesman of an oral tradition running through indefinite centuries, his mind filled with inherited formulas and themes.

Ionia in the eighth century? The very idea of any definite time and place is incompatible with these theories. And yet the focus of time and place is quite essential here. Indeed, no distinctive event of any importance can be conceived apart from its crucial occasion. If it were so conceived, it would become an abstraction, or we would take things for granted and invoke habit, custom, tradition. Any serious achievement must have its moment of intensity as well as a point of contact with reality.

Ionia of the eighth century must thus be connected with Homer in spirit, and not only as a matter of historical record. But how can this be done? It need not deter us that no evidence exists contemporary with Homer. With our eyes upon what happened a century or two later, we may try to realize the intellectual climate of that age. What matters here is not any reference to alleged facts or even formulation of definite ideas, but an unstated implicit philosophy. The very style of Homer suggests a mode of perceiving reality that is in tune with what we know of early Ionia. Thought and art all at once conspired to make the poems what they are.

IV

What relevance to Homer do we find, then, in early Ionia? Thence came much that was to distinguish art, literature, and philosophy elsewhere in Greece. From Ionian islands (e.g., Delos, Samos, Naxos, Paros) come many of the earliest *kouroi*—those male nudes which, in an upright figure, so delicately arrest a moment of poise expressing both stillness and movement. At Miletus in the seventh to sixth centuries arose that philosophy which, with Thales, Anaximander, and Anaximenes, imaginatively interpreted matter or reality, tracing it back to one principle, and thus saw an animate force at work through the realm of nature. In Ionia lived the first historians who looked at events in terms of their impact upon cities and people.

Here is a common trend. Here is what we may call the Ionian spirit. It is turned toward the outer world. It is secular, objective, keenly perceptive, and yet, at the same time, filled with wonder. Those early statues, while expressing the momentary vitality of a human body, are removed from everyday realism: no wonder that they may be interpreted both as young athletes and as Apollos. Those Ionian philosophers tried to account for what they actually saw and yet felt in the multiplicity of things the presence of one unfathomable force. Those early historians were concerned with events yet impressed with genealogies that carry through time the baffling impact of a god, a hero, a family, or a city.

Keen perception and unbounded wonder—these indeed are qualities that may be found at any time, whenever lucidity and deep interest blend. But what characterizes a creative moment of history is the pervasive impact of one initial touch. The same deep imprint abides in a variety of instances. There is the sense of a widespread discovery. An idea, an intuition flashes out, reverberates, extends abroad in countless kindred forms.

Thus, in Ionia and in early Greece, one *kouros* shows all the distinction of a unique, lifelike moment, but the same type is rehearsed in many other instances without losing any of its freshness. Similarly, the philosophical intuition of one creative plastic principle could be tested again and again in the realm of nature. Even the efforts of the logographers (or early historians) revealed a method which might be universally applicable from place to place. Everywhere the typical sprang directly from the perception of life. What we are presented with is not a family resemblance such as we commonly find in things of the same provenance, but, rather, a newly perceived identity in things scattered the world over. The type was here at one with a truth persistently perceived.

Now these remarks can be applied to Homer as well as to Ionia. For the high degree in which such qualities are shown is eminently Homeric. We find in the poems the same sharp perception and the same pervasive wonder, the focus on single things and the universalizing approach, the singular and the typical. As in the statues, there is a strong sense of position in the human figure; as in the philosophers, the animate force running through all nature. Although these views or insights can be found elsewhere, they are here manifest with a particular intensity. Why is it, for instance, that Homer is regarded by some as deeply religious because his gods are continually involved in the action, while others consider him quite secular because he seems to use the "divine machinery" as a mere mode of representation? The reason lies in the way the observation of nature so persistently blends with a sense of mystery. The resilience of a body appeared to Homer as miraculous as it was real; so what more natural than that a god might seem to sustain it? "All things are full of gods," said Thales.

Or consider the idea of an animate force one and the same throughout nature. We see it especially in the similes. It seems directly named in the word *menos*, which indicates the native might of the elements as well as of a man or any animal. In *Il.* 14.394, the roaring surge of sea and fire and wind is likened to that of an army: compare the elements of air, water, and fire as discussed by the philosophers. It is surely not far-

fetched to suppose that the wonder of these dramatic perceptions had something to do with the rise of Ionian philosophy.

V

Or we may look at Ionia, more generally, from a geo-
graphic and historical point of view. Here were a people settled in a new land: behind them, to the west, was their
ancestral home, once the seat of Mycenaean civilization; and
before them, to the east, lay Anatolia, Assyria, Mesopotamia,
Egypt—all lands that had witnessed, or were still witnessing,
civilizations far more ancient than the Mycenaean.

Imagine now the situation of a people so removed from
traditional pieties and loyalties and faced with broad new perspectives. We have neither an empire nor a single-minded
city-state nor a tribal society; what we have, rather, is many
city-states emerging, opening up, seeking their bearings on
the verge of a new world—both a place attained and a sense
of outlying spaces, the self-assertion of settlers and the free
spirit of travelers, traders, adventurers. There was no room,
therefore, for any nationalistic or parochial narrowness; the
circumstances themselves favored an open mind, a readiness
to perceive, absorb, and assimilate. No wonder that Herodo-
tus, with his international outlook and world-ranging sym-
pathies, came from here. Much of what later characterized
Athens was here in embryo, not yet crystallized into the patterns of a powerful state and expanding in greater sympathy
with the world at large.

We may relate Homer to these conditions. Consider his
universal view of mankind (as shown, for instance, in the
famous simile of the leaves, *Il.* 6.146ff.); the lack of bias; the
avoidance of any narrow ethnic descriptions; the glorious epithets he bestows upon all peoples near and far; and, above
all, the fact that he puts Greeks and Trojans on the same

human level. The influence of the East, an influence whose details remain unknown, must have concurred with poetry in fostering this sense of relativity and universality. The very awareness of other great civilizations was such as to give pause to the inquiring mind. In a place so exposed to the cross-currents of the world, and in such a period of transition, any hallowed glory must have yielded to the feeling that any one country is only part of a wider reality.

There was, on the other hand, the Mycenaean past, the ancestral glory made more wonderful by the memory of its fall. Here lay the subject matter of the poems. Nor was it merely a question of subject matter. The Minoan civilization, with its Mycenaean offshoot, had left a splendid heritage. Homer knew it; and he let this splendor be reflected in the palaces of Alcinous and Menelaus, a joy to the eyes of visiting Odysseus and Telemachus (*Od.* 7.84ff., 4.43ff.).

But Mycenaean opulence is a distant glow in Homer. Ionia and the whole Greek world were quite removed from it in the Homeric age. We may contrast with the exuberance of Cretan and Mycenaean vase-paintings the "Geometric" vases of the ninth to late eighth centuries, to whose designs Homer's compositional patterns have been compared. Abstract form, linear or circular rhythms here prevail and subdue any figurative shape. What stands out is measure, outline for its own sake.

Geometric clarity, like form or rhythm, is certainly relevant to Homer. But the Homeric achievement is far more complex, the Ionian background far richer (we may suppose) than what we may learn from the patterned arrangements of the Geometric style. We should look at the imagery itself, as well as at the arrangement or the composition. Something of Cretan or Minoan sensuousness remains in those vibrant geometric lines which here and there recompose the human or

animal figure; and the way movement is resolved into life
might make us think of Homer, as when, for instance, he sees
in the curling crest of a wave the same shape or impact as
that of a man surging in action.

But at this point it becomes impossible to project definite
historical influences into the vital Homeric touch, which has
its own insoluble integrity. We can only point to the way in
which seemingly opposed qualities are at once integrated in
the unity of the actual expression: richness and simplicity of
form, lingering fullness and rapidity, intensity and restraint.
The problem is one of values. We can only draw closer to the
historical Homer by trying to see how these values were in-
tuited and realized rather than by deriving them from something else.

VI

What we have gleaned from history is really internal to
the poems themselves. The signals of age and place point to
Homer by suggesting Homeric qualities and, by the same token, Homer sheds light upon the historical circumstances. We
must imagine eighth-century Ionia both as a real country and
as an ideal place, both as an actual community of people and
as a focal point for the rise and growth of Homeric poetry.

Since it was a matter of both popular success and achievement, we may ask: what was it that stirred the imagination
of a whole people? What force of persuasion inspired the poet
and won over his listeners? What art proved so genuine in
itself and yet so popular? And how did this process find its
way?

A poet sang; others listened, wondered, were inspired
in turn; the news spread. A happening as simple as this, and
as unfathomable, as elusive. It escapes both historical re-

search and abstract theory. We can only try to conjure up sympathetically a place, an occasion. Even the most momentous spiritual developments can be traced back to some concrete setting: a meeting, a dialogue, any form of common experience. Here "time concurs with place and place with time." What has been brooding in the individual mind finds its way out. There is communion, revelation, enlightenment. The social world comes into the picture. A flash of the imagination broadens into the spirit of the age. In the case of Homer, poetic thought found a style and the style became pervasive. The success was one with the achievement itself; and it contained, in embryo, the poet's posthumous glory.

Success, acclaim—we can imagine the word-of-mouth fame of those days: a certain poet suddenly extolled, his words repeated, learnt, and inspiring other poetic energies in their turn. Here was novelty, surprise, wonder. No mere question of an epic subject matter appealing, as anywhere else, to the audience, no mere question of agreeable or exciting stories. We are driven back to our first point, to that striking impression of truth in the Homeric representation, something that appeals even to the untutored child. What stands out uppermost is the form of his art. The reasons that ensured Homer's first triumph were essentially the same as those which still sustain him today in the eyes of the reader; all other factors (for example, that he embodies the epic tradition or sang national glories) are quite secondary and can be applied to many others. There is, in any work of art, an intimate quality that justifies its vital appeal over and above any cultural incrustation.

Therefore let us look again at the form of Homer's art in terms of its appeal to the public, insofar as it steadily gained ground and stirred a response which, in turn, gave further range to the initial poetic impulse. The listeners themselves, aware or not, were won over by that sense of truth which, in the poet, precipitated the compositional process.

What, more particularly, was the secret that so opened the world to Homer's poetry? It lay in the way the story was presented, in the way the whole action of the poems was rendered in the rhythm of consecutive moments that make up a limited series of days (see chap. 2). Such a treatment of time both informed the style of the succeeding sentences and told the story in terms of an unfolding experience. Any complex event might thus be resolved into the creative moments of its realization.

Time, unwittingly, entered the world of art. It was the time of human experience, not any mythical entity. Unnamed, scarcely realized or singled out for its own sake, the sense of time ran like lifeblood through the narrative material. It thus hardly amounted to any fixed idea. It was, rather, at one with a concrete feeling for events, one with the bare realization of how anything happens, takes place, exists, passes away. Henceforward no storied or legendary fact could be taken for granted. It had to be rendered in the actual pulse of its happening.

The effect must have been tremendous. A new clarity emerged. Things far and near, great and small, solemn and familiar could now be seen in the same light. Time was the great catalyst. For on the pure level of coming and going or of being and passing away, everything mentioned appeared to enjoy its pertinent portion of a common existence. In the bright, lingering moment a god or hero or animal appeared to breathe the same air—hence, in the similes, the same momentary stress bringing different worlds together. Hence any episode, however marvelous, reduced to those moments which make it seem possible, convincing, forcible—as when

Achilles' incipient attack on Agamemnon is thwarted by Athena, who simply stands behind him clasping his hair (*Il.* 1.199):

> and amazed was Achilles, / he turned and instantly
>   knew
> the goddess Pallas Athena, / and dread was the light in
>   her eyes.

Here is no glorious epiphany, but a touch, a turn, a shock of recognition, a kindling glance—each act an inevitable moment.

The intellectual and philosophical implications were momentous. The style had its own poetic logic. So forceful was the rhythm of these continuous moments that anything inconsistent with their vital movement tended to be discarded. As if it were a natural law, an instinctive sense of time proportioned any event to the span of what anyone might experience. Hence the abridgment of anything purely mythical or fantastic; hence the focus upon sheer happening rather than curiosity or variety of incidents. The material was thus simplified yet enriched with an inward stress. Sentence followed upon sentence as did moment upon moment, dynamically moving forward and leaving out any unnecessary accretion. The pulse of time, while alike in every case, gave each happening the sense of a newly won vantage point, as though stagnant waters were made to flow, revealing in the whorls of their current the incidents of the riverbed. We may again be reminded of the way the Ionian philosophers both simplified and dramatized the world's existence by positing at its source one basic and pervasive element.

Or we may look at the achievement of this style in purely visual terms. For Homer visualizes any passing occurrence; and such visualization is not any voluntary or pointed effect brought out here and there, but an essential element of Homeric art.

Here again the sense of time is most relevant. For what stands out is the concrete perception of a thing as intrinsic to the moment that brings it into play. The act evokes an image, the image is only there on the strength of that act. Truth to life lies in a figure so caught in its moment of resilience.

It is not, therefore, a matter of merely observing and reproducing objective details. It is a question of touch. But what is this touch, what kind of principle does it imply? It is seeing form in the movement, movement in the form. It is a sense of lightness in the weight, of weight in the lightness. It means catching the lifelike moment of an image and holding it for just as long as the heartbeat lasts. It ultimately harks back to a native yearning for form and yet to transcend that form. Position and motion materialize in an object only to let it go the next instant. Things are presented as modes of being.

It is as if the pulse of time (which is life) vivified any objective figure (which is matter) and, vice versa, objects gave focus and solidity to the passage of time. Hence, in Homer, there is no character but he or she is presented (or imagined) as a body, no body but filled with life and seen in the action of a pertinent organ or limb. Even a solitary hand that clasps or releases a spear gives us a sense of self-contained power. We may again be reminded of early Greek statuary—how vital (much more so than in a modern work) appears even a fragmentary torso or foot or hand—quite apart from who it belongs to. The vivid instance makes any narrow identification seem unimportant. It is, ultimately, for this reason that Homer does not usually introduce his characters when they first appear. They simply stand out all at once. Time is necessarily impartial; and any explanation would undermine the resilience of the rising moment.

VII

Let us now turn again to the historical side of the problem, the actual rise of Homeric poetry in eighth-century Ionia,
and this time from the viewpoint of style insofar as it affects
the composition from sentence to sentence, passage to passage.

This style, it is clear, should not be explained away as a
primitive "parataxis" (or mere coordination of sentences) by
opposing an earlier simplicity to a later complexity. No, the
syntax itself has its own distinctive poetic reason in highlighting the moment and sustaining the continuous stream of time.
In this respect, the Homeric poems are as different from later
works as they are, say, from Gilgamesh or the Indian epics.
Everywhere else we find the complex fortunes of nations and
individuals; here, a linear development and the sharp thrust
of action upon action.

Even less shall we see in this style the technique of the
"oral poet" who, in his need to perform instantly, cannot
think ahead and must mention one thing at a time. Homer's
bright focus on single moments would here be interpreted
quite negatively as an incapacity to think beyond the object
at hand.

Just as the achievement was sui generis, so were the conditions of the time. We must, above all, envisage a period of
concentration: poetic activities gathering momentum, a unison of art and thought reaching its climax, the very craft of
verse coming into harmony with the ferment of ideas. How
long was this period of concentration? Long enough to allow
for the assimilation of the expressive material but short
enough to account for a sense of urgency and intensity—not
necessarily more than three generations. We might compare
other high points of poetic activity: the time of Shakespeare

or of Greek tragedy. There is always a swift development, at once intensity and fullness of production.

We must thus imagine a renaissance, not the last breath of an epic tradition but a new beginning. The epic subject matter still prevailed but was seen in a new light. Gods and heroes were brought down to earth, humanized, mellowed, and transformed into characters; myths were divested of their fantastic elements, made into human stories, seen as events actually taking place; dispensations of the gods or designs of fate had to find a responsive counterpoint in the promptings of the human mind and no longer be taken for granted. Individual emotion or thought was coming into its own. Lyric poetry was only a step away. When a Homeric hero addresses his own heart, he makes us think of Archilochus.

In what circumstances did this new approach work upon the preexisting material? Ionians and Aeolians had brought with them from the Greek mainland Mycenaean legends and, we may suppose, Mycenaean poetry. Here were the sources (for where else could they be?) of much mythical knowledge that we find later. Comprehensive narratives were available, out of which only the scattered imagery of outstanding moments makes its appearance in Greek poetry: in Homer, for instance, there is nothing of Hecuba's dream or Paris' judgment, but, out of the whole cycle, only a final dramatic episode. A process of poetic choices was thus afoot. On what grounds was it carried out? Homer himself gives us a clue when he presents his bards of the *Odyssey,* Phemius and Demodocus, singing songs that touch the heart to the quick (*Od.* 1.325ff.; 8.73ff., 499ff.). "That song do people most glorify which is the newest to float round those who hear it," says Telemachus (*Od.* 1.351ff.); and we must give the word *newest* a pregnant sense—not only novelty of subject matter but the way the emotions are freshly stirred. What Telemachus un-

derstands as novelty of topic is, in a deeper sense, novelty of
conception. "Let your heart and soul dare to listen," he goes
on to say, "not Odysseus alone in Troy was denied the day
of return; many others there were that have perished"; and
he seems to explain what he means: the song and what
haunts the mind are one. How significant, in this context, is
the emphasis on the doom of one and all, of Odysseus and
others!—experience juxtaposed to experience, moment to moment on the strength of a central human interest. Indeed,
many, at any time, might feel their own plight here. The poetry appears very consistent with a style so absorbed in the
presentation of crucial human moments.

Hence a swift realization into form: the narrative material
is dramatized, either resolved into dialogue or into immediate
instants of experienced time. The artistic activity must have
been relentless, pervasive: poems no sooner conceived than
brought out, poems continually recited in the marketplace or
in private houses; poems echoing one another on the strength
of a common quality. And we may imagine, along with this
activity, the sense of discovery or intellectual enthusiasm in
so bringing the gods down to earth and breathing life into
hallowed material gone stale. To get an idea of the impetus,
we may think of other periods of transformation closer to us,
the fourteenth century in Florence, for instance, when Giotto
and his school similarly brought out a new immediacy of form
over and above the Byzantine tradition.

How radical this process of transformation was is especially shown by the language itself. The very means of expression were very swiftly assimilated to an art form in which
even an obscure archaic phrase could find a new function in
delivering the succession of lifelike acts. Old and new, vernacular and foreign here found a common ground. That as-
similating trend which always occurs in any language was

now intensified, quickened by the prompting of art. Hence the wealth of forms and of heterogeneous words in the Homeric poems. The fact that the language shows a mixture of dialects is significant in this respect. It has usually been regarded as evidence of a conventional epic idiom whose formation required centuries; but we should, rather, point out its immediate relevance to the art of the times. For the need of poetic expression was paramount. It could not be held to the peculiar idioms of one vernacular. It had to expand, finding its own form. What particular words or phrases could it rely upon? The ultimate suggestion was given by the rhythm that appeared so intrinsic to the rendering of successive acts, each of them enjoying its moment of suspense before passing away like a sound floating through the air.

Irregularities harmonized, discrepancies of dialect fused into one all-encompassing whole—here again are symptoms of an intensified effort in poetic expression, and not of a long tradition. We must thus imagine somewhere in Ionia a center, a strong poetic nucleus, a point of both attraction and diffusion; thence came a language or a style which had a natural instinct to transcend any local boundary and universalize the forms of expression, in tune with that poetic ideal implicit in Homeric poetry. Again we might draw analogies: the way, for instance, in which the Florentine dialect was universalized through the work of Dante.

Homer was at home in eighth-century Ionia. Are we, then, to consider Homer as the sole author of both the *Iliad* and the *Odyssey*? I believe it is so. But the bare fact of authorship, in its literal sense, is unimportant. We are too influenced by the idea of attribution and copyright. A work of art is no private domain. It is, indeed, its high distinction that anyone, if endowed with sympathetic insight, can make it his or her own.

What matters, rather, is to recognize in a work of art a principle of perception and expression. Such a principle naturally reveals itself in a distinctive individual touch. Herein lies a nameless originality whose ingredients (whatever they are) cannot be concocted, faked, or manipulated. At the same time, however, it is not a question of an exclusive personal stamp. The poetic value here envisaged would not be what it is unless it could be communicated and cast abroad. It is by nature pervasive, or magnetic. Thus more than one person may be imbued with the same spirit; the master's touch may pass to the followers without losing its integrity. What matters is a power of thought which can neither be lightly improvised nor laboriously conjured up.

The problem of who exactly was the great inventive genius is secondary. We should, rather, see the genius in the work itself and recognize an original distinctive core of poetic thought and meaning, avoiding the fallacy of looking at the matter from a merely anthropological or historical viewpoint and thus losing the sense of any distinctive value as the primary cause of the phenomenon itself. What we need is neither hero-worship nor emphasis on mere cultural influences, but recognition of a certain creative principle finding its way in time and place—a principle which, though difficult to analyze, is no less momentous in its factual impact.

Homer is thus the driving force behind the poems, but there is no need to ascribe to him every part of them. At the same time, however, his touch is everywhere. In the same way, Shakespeare's hand can be felt in all three parts of *Henry VI*, although the play is not completely his own. The question of authorship is, finally, one of intensity. It is up to us whether we ascribe an inferior passage to an inferior hand or to a lapse on the part of the same original author. We might say that in the *Iliad* and the *Odyssey* the great dialogues (like the one between Hector and Andromache) are most distinctly Homeric on the strength of their outright dramatization, or the battle scenes because of their tight representation from moment to moment; while, by the same account, we might consider less Homeric the long narratives of Nestor or the mythical accounts of the heroines in Hades. The more we think of it, the more the question of authorship becomes a question of quality.

The question remains of how the poems were produced, published, made known to the world—a question complicated by the assumption that no knowledge of writing existed in Homer's time. This assumption depends upon a negative argument, in view of the fact that there is no evidence of any inscription belonging to that age and area, nor is there any clear, explicit mention of writing in the poems themselves.

Writing had, however, existed in the Mycenaean world and throughout the Near East for hundreds of years, as attested by many inscriptions. It is therefore hard to believe that the troubled times following the fall of Mycenae were characterized by total illiteracy. It is hard, at least, to believe that the very idea of writing had been lost and that, if the idea was present in people's minds, it could not actually have been implemented.

But let us suppose that no writing existed. Against the analysts who believed in the conflation of shorter poems, we may find support in the theories of oral composition that have shown how great the powers of human memory can be. Should we, then, consider Homer a "monumental composer" who so mastered the craft of his predecessors and perfected it to such a degree that he could deliver, from performance to performance, the whole extent of the poems?

The case of Homer and eighth-century Ionia appears to be different. The lack of writing certainly increased the power of memory and associated talents; but we should again invoke the distinctive form of Homeric poetry and look at that form insofar as it appealed to the retentive faculties of the mind.

If we had a narrative filled with adventure or intrigue or curious details, its claim on memory would indeed be formidable, for we would then have to come to terms with a discursive or wayward material refractory to any basic form of thought. But the case of Homer is quite the opposite. The narrative throughout is simplified into essential instances of action, whence a typical beat, a fundamental pattern, an imagery whose details but reinforce the recurring outline. Form reigns supreme; and it is a form of thought as well as of style.

It was therefore not a question of memorizing. The strain placed on memory was as much as possible absorbed into the activity of thought. To remember a long stretch of poetry was to be immersed again and again in a certain mode of perception, to realize again and again a certain form of expression. In the end there might be little difference between remembering and composing anew; for the form of representation proved to be universally applicable to the most diverse material, as though a tune were conceived ever waiting for words in order to be put into song. But the tune here was no less than the tune of action—that is to say, the mental image of a pattern or a rhythm in the flow of any happening from moment to moment.

The immediate preservation of the poems must be seen in the same light. Imagine, again, the fervor of the times. The words of the poet fell on minds equally receptive and retentive. No question of an audience merely wishing to be entertained. The poet and his listeners, we suppose, were sharing the same experience. The general interest lay not so much in a good story as in its mode of delivery. The poetic strain ran through the listeners themselves, gathering them into the task of retention, inscribing the poems in their minds before they were written down.

As to how the work itself grew in the poet's mind and achieved its final form, that must forever remain a mystery. But isn't it always?

BIBLIOGRAPHY

Translations

The free poetic translations of George Chapman (1616) and of Alexander Pope (1726) still convey the power of Homer. The poet William Cullen Bryant (*Iliad*, 1870; *Odyssey*, 1871) gives us a clear, competent version in blank verse. A. Lang, W. Leaf, and E. Myers for the *Iliad* and S. H. Butcher and A. Lang for the *Odyssey* (1879), produced close versions in high-wrought prose. The poetic idiom of our time is best achieved by Robert Fitzgerald (*Odyssey*, 1961; *Iliad*, 1974). Richard Lattimore (*Iliad*, 1951; *Odyssey*, 1967) is both very readable and quite literal; his verses correspond to those of the original. E. V. Rieu (*Odyssey*, 1946; *Iliad*, 1951) will appeal to those who wish to read the poems as a straightforward story written in current modern prose.

The following works are listed in chronological order.

On Homeric criticism

J. L. Myres. *Homer and his Critics*. London, 1958.
Howard Clarke. *Homer's Readers*. Newark, 1981.

Works more directly concerned with poetry than with background

S. E. Bassett. *The Poetry of Homer*. Berkeley, 1938.
Rachel Bespaloff. *De l'Iliade*. New York, 1943. Translated by Mary McCarthy as *On the Iliad*. Washington, D.C., 1947.
Simone Weil. *L'Iliade ou le poème de la force*. Marseille, 1947. Translated by Mary McCarthy as *The Iliad: or, the Poem of Force*. Wallingford, Penna., 1957.
Gabriel Germain. *Homère*. Paris, 1958. Translated by Richard Howard as *Homer*. New York, 1960.

Paolo Vivante. *The Homeric Imagination: A Study of Homer's Poetic Perception of Reality.* Bloomington, Ind., 1970. Reprint New York, 1983.

Norman Austin. *Archery at the Dark of the Moon: Poetic Problems in Homer's Odyssey.* Berkeley, 1975.

John H. Finley. *Homer's Odyssey.* Cambridge, Mass., 1978.

Jasper Griffin. *Homer on Life and Death.* Oxford, 1980.

INDEX

Achilles: wrath of, 1–2, 37, 63; image of, 9, 21, 60–61; humanization of, 58–60; as a character, 58–74; and sense of time, 62–63; aloofness of, 63; and Patroclus, 64, 67; and Priam, 64–65, 68–70; inner power of, 65, 66; his refusal to eat, 67; consistency of, 71–72; conventional view of, 73; and Diomedes, 74; mentioned, 18, 38

Action: voluminous, 23, 25; and existence, 26–32, 41; perspicuity of, 46–47

Aeneid, 45

Aeschylus, 85, 108

Aesthetic values: and human values, 69, 147; perception of, 102

Agamemnon, 79–84; cruelty, weakness of, 82; heroic mold of, 82

Ajax, 47–50; and idea of resistance, 48–49; silence of, 50; mentioned, 149

Alcaeus, 85

Alcinous: garden of, 178–80

Allegory, 112

Anaximander, 196

Anaximenes, 196

Andromache, 4–5; and Hector, 53–54

Animal nature: and man, 153, 155

Animate energy, 149; and character, 150, 151; and view of reality, 197–98

Anthropological approach, 43

Anticlea (mother of Odysseus), 108

Aphrodite: and Helen, 92–95

Apollo: image of, 1; and Achilles, 70; and Diomedes, 75, 77

Archilochus, 192, 206

Aristotle, 19, 108

Artemis, 135

Asius: and Hector, 57; mentioned, 142

Assemblies, 193

Ate, 84

Athena: image of, 7; nature of her influence, 33, 124, 136; and Diomedes, 74–76; and Odysseus, 109–12; and Telemachus, 137–39

Battle scenes: and plot, 24; individuality of, 141

Beauty: moment of, 33, 124; and sense of the concrete, 176; and awe, 176–77, 181, 182; and luxuriance, 179–80

Body: parts of, 30, 149–51, 154–55; not opposed to mind, 166

Callinus, 192

Calypso, 107, 140; cave of, 177–80

Cayster (river), 161, 194

Chapman, G., 122

Character: and action, 45–46, 55, 72, 81, 82, 97; fundamental sense of, 46, 79, 96, 113; and idiosyncrasies, 55; Homeric and post-Homeric treatment of, 83–84, 85, 97; and vitality of the image, 103

Child: and Homer, 1, 3, 8, 201

Chios, 194

Chryses, 1, 2–3, 80

215

DATE DUE